CCCC STUDIES IN WRITING & RHETORIC

Edited by Victor Villanueva, Washington State University

The aim of the CCCC Studies in Writing & Rhetoric Series is to influence how we think about language in action and especially how writing gets taught at the college level. The methods of studies vary from the critical to historical to linguistic to ethnographic, and their authors draw on work in various fields that inform composition—including rhetoric, communication, education, discourse analysis, psychology, cultural studies, and literature. Their focuses are similarly diverse—ranging from individual writers and teachers, to work on classrooms and communities and curricula, to analyses of the social, political, and material contexts of writing and its teaching.

SWR was one of the first scholarly book series to focus on the teaching of writing. It was established in 1980 by the Conference on College Composition and Communication (CCCC) in order to promote research in the emerging field of writing studies. As our field has grown, the research sponsored by SWR has continued to articulate the commitment of CCCC to supporting the work of writing teachers as reflective practitioners and intellectuals.

We are eager to identify influential work in writing and rhetoric as it emerges. We thus ask authors to send us project proposals that clearly situate their work in the field and show how they aim to redirect our ongoing conversations about writing and its teaching. Proposals should include an overview of the project, a brief annotated table of contents, and a sample chapter. They should not exceed 10,000 words.

To submit a proposal, please register as an author at www.editorial manager.com/nctebp. Once registered, follow the steps to submit a proposal (be sure to choose SWR Book Proposal from the drop-down list of article submission types).

RHETORIC OF RESPECT

RECOGNIZING CHANGE AT A COMMUNITY WRITING CENTER

Tiffany Rousculp
Salt Lake Community College

Conference on College Composition and Communication

National Council of Teachers of English

Staff Editor: Bonny Graham
Series Editor: Victor Villanueva
Interior Design: Mary Rohrer
Cover Design: Mary Rohrer and Lynn Weckhorst

NCTE Stock Number: 41472

It is the policy of NCTE in its journals and other publications to provide a forum for the open discussion of ideas concerning the content and the teaching of English and the language arts. Publicity accorded to any particular point of view does not imply endorsement by the Executive Committee, the Board of Directors, or the membership at large, except in announcements of policy, where such endorsement is clearly specified.

Every effort has been made to provide current URLs and email addresses, but because of the rapidly changing nature of the Web, some sites and addresses may no longer be accessible.

Publication partially funded by a subvention grant from the Conference on College Composition and Communication of the National Council of Teachers of English.

Library of Congress Cataloging-in-Publication Data
Rousculp, Tiffany, 1968-
  Rhetoric of respect : recognizing change at a community writing center / Tiffany Rousculp, Salt Lake Community College.
    pages cm. — (Studies in Writing and Rhetoric)
  Includes bibliographical references and index.
  ISBN 978-0-8141-4147-2 (pbk : alk. paper)
  1. English language—Rhetoric—Study and teaching. 2. Report writing—Study and teaching (Higher). 3. Writing centers—Administration. I. Title.
  PE1404.R679 2014
  808'.0420711—dc23
                                                            2013040397

This book is for Harold Davis Richardson.
Grandpa, thank you for the hand-me-down genes; I hope I have
worn them well.

CONTENTS

Writers who enter Cooper's web are most often subsumed by it, and ultimately, most often acclimate to it in order to survive. Others, however, may also resist the web, shake it, build new threads, start new webs.
—Sidney I. Dobrin and Christian R. Weisser,
Natural Discourse: Toward Ecocomposition

I HAVE TO SAY, THIS BOOK IS NOT THE ONE I intended to write. As the founding director of a community writing center where the words *reflect* and *revise* are etched two-feet high across the front windows, I look forward to changing my texts and find comfort in my "heavy reviser" writing process. Moreover, I know that when writing for publication, rarely, if ever, does an end product look like what the author initially imagined. So, while I'm not surprised at this book's transformations, I want to draw attention to its unruly story because it echoes the tumultuous evolution of the Community Writing Center (CWC) sponsored by Salt Lake Community College (SLCC) since 2001.

Life does not follow predictable patterns. It surprises and disappoints; it veers and stabilizes—it pushes boundaries and finds stasis. The life of the SLCC Community Writing Center has been no exception. Therefore, instead of trying to draw a neat set of conclusions about what the CWC was,[1] what the CWC's partnerships with more than 5,000 community members meant, or what the CWC's relationships with more than 130 community organizations should mean to the fields of rhetoric, composition, writing centers, and community literacy studies, I want to take you on a path through its uncertainty and malleability. In doing so, I seek not to *define* "change" as it happened at the CWC, but instead to *recognize* it and the possibilities that it opens for literacy learning. But, first, let me tell you about this book. . . .

I started writing this book (if you accept that thinking about writing is writing) in 2006 with the CWC's then-assistant director, Melissa Helquist. We knew that the CWC was an important part of the overlapping stories of rhetoric, composition, writing centers, and community literacy; we also knew that we needed to write it together in order to honor the center's collaborative environment and practices. However, publisher reception to our queries at a Conference on College Composition and Communication (CCCC) convention was muted: they believed an audience for a book about a community writing center was thin at best. We returned to Salt Lake with the intention to carry forward in our project, but academic life and love intervened when Helquist moved to Canada a year later for her husband's postdoc appointment. We agreed that we'd try to collaborate long distance, though we both knew the odds of that happening were slim since Helquist would no longer be involved with the CWC's work.

The following year, I was determined to get something substantial about the Community Writing Center into print. I'd written articles for publications such as *Reflections*, the *Writing Lab Newsletter*, and the *Writing Center Director's Resource Book* and had presented at dozens of conferences—but still, I thought the SLCC Community Writing Center warranted a book project. It had been growing for seven years and had collaborated with thousands of people; further, I was starting to hear from scholars at academic institutions who wanted advice on starting their own community writing center projects. I appealed to my department chair and my dean for a small bit of time reassigned from teaching so I could focus only on directing the CWC and writing a book. They granted me one year away from my normal teaching load.

Even though I'd be writing the book on my own—without Helquist—I could not imagine filling it with my words only. The discourses that created the Community Writing Center were so varied—academic, nonacademic, communal, personal, activist, reflective, pragmatic—that I wanted to mimic their mosaic-ness in a publication highlighting multiple voices. I imagined a collage of writings that I would coordinate with my own words, imitating the way I had directed the center. I put out an open call for contributions to community members, partners, volunteers, and current and previous staff. A handful of submissions trickled in: two from Advisory Committee members, three from volunteers, one from a writer, and several from a CWC writing assistant, Chanel Earl. Earl sent me multiple short pieces, one of which was a prose poem about writers at the CWC, with snapshots of one writer, Daryl, woven throughout it:

Daryl #1

Daryl came in during the summer. He smelled like cigarettes and alcohol, and he spoke with a slur. I helped him register as a writer with us, even though our database said he had been in before. He didn't give us a phone number because he didn't have one. He wanted to write a memoir, and he wanted to talk about it. After we talked, I gave him a pad of paper. "This is for you," I said. "Start writing your memoir and when you have a few pages written bring them back in and we can help you with them." He came back the next day with several pages. He had written a sad and dark summary of his early life. It was honest. "Good job," I said. We talked about which stories he could expand on. He came back the next week with more pages. He came back several more times, and then he disappeared.

Daryl #2

Daryl came in during the winter. He smelled like cigarettes and spoke with a slur. Chris helped him register as a writer with us. This time he gave us a phone number. He said he now had a medical bed at the shelter. He had just left the hospital where he had surgery and they told him not to drink anymore. He lost his backpack one night when he had a seizure in the park and was rushed to the hospital without it. He had lost his memoir. Chris gave him a journal to write in, and she offered to keep a copy of all his writing at the center. He began to write. He came back the next day, and the next, and sometimes he fell asleep in one of our comfortable chairs. He came back the next week with pages to copy. He came back several more times, and then disappeared.

Daryl #3
Daryl came in during the spring. He smelled like medicine and soap, and he smiled as he spoke. "I haven't forgotten you guys," he said. "I wanted to come by and let you know I am still writing." He was excited. "And that things are changing at the shelter. People have seen that I am changing and they think, 'if that guy can go clean, I can.'" He patted himself on the back. "This is for you. Without you guys I don't know how much of this I would have been able to do." He didn't come in again.

Contributions from others—"Adult Literacy," "On Writing," "I Write," "Storytelling"—were each compelling in their own way and depicted the mixture of people and voices at the CWC. It was exciting, though I was starting to doubt my ability to form something cohesive from them. I never had a chance to try, because financial crisis struck (as it did for many during the 2008 national recession) and all efforts had to turn to minimizing damage to the CWC. Frantic and fierce counterarguments to administrative decisions, unprecedented local and national declarations of support, and strategic appeals ended well for the center. Even so, time to write remained elusive during my final year as director, which was filled with an increased teaching load and the responsibility to ready the center for a new director by shoring up the CWC's stability and making clear its essential value to both Salt Lake Community College and the Salt Lake community.

When I left in May 2010, after twelve years with the Community Writing Center, it was finally time to write this book. With a sabbatical ahead of me, I settled into my on-campus office and got down to it. Through a mixture of nostalgia and anticipation, I realized that I had to be separate from the Community Writing Center in order to reflect on and write about it. Leaning back in my chair, gazing past the parking lot and brick walls of the community college's urban campus, I could see the Wasatch Mountains that frame the east edge of the Salt Lake valley. Rust and yellow leaves covered them, though that would change into snow, and then again to deep, glowing spring green while I wrote. In this silent solitary space, I sorted through twelve years of activity, experience, documents, memories, and chaos, trying to make meaning to share with colleagues in rhetoric, composition, writing centers, and community literacy.

Even though the book would now be written by a single author and stand as my interpretation of the CWC (rather than a collage of voices), I was still committed to replicating the center's ideologies in what I wrote; to that end, I focused on accessibility. The decisions I made at the CWC were always grounded in creating and maintaining access—for the community and for the staff members. Likewise, I insisted that what I wrote about the center be accessible to anyone who is or may have been a part of the CWC. Therefore, I would not write a "regular" academic text, as I detailed in an earlier draft:

> As I have written this book, I have been continually mindful of readers outside of composition, and even those outside academia, though they may not constitute a significant audience. The purpose of the SLCC Community Writing Center has been to provide access to fluid and respectful learning opportunities for the community; to write in a way that prevents such access would contradict the purpose of the past decade of my working life.

Accordingly, I wrote for an extremely broad, imaginary audience and tried to blend explanations of basic academic concepts (e.g., "disciplines," "discourse," "pedagogy") with theoretical argument. I shared my work with my husband, Chris Lippard (an academic outside of composition), and my mother, Bev Rousculp (a determinedly nonacademic person), to make sure that people outside of my field—and outside the academy—could understand it. They could—and they liked it.

I began submitting queries to publishers once I had completed a full manuscript. By then, community literacy work had cast its net wider and interest was high. Several publications (Goldblatt, *Because*; Flower, *Community*; Parks; Long; Rose and Weiser; and Ackerman and Coogan, *Public Work*, among others) had deepened scholarship into this amorphous, yet somehow related, field of work that the SLCC Community Writing Center belonged to. Institutions including the University of New Mexico and Auburn University had opened their own community writing centers. Other programs were emerging as well, and I happily talked with them, offering encouragement and support. The timing for an in-depth look at the SLCC Community Writing Center seemed right.

Yet my book wasn't "right." My envisioned audience of academic and nonacademic readers was a fantasy. The only people likely to want to read such a book were compositionists, and as much as I wanted to open access to anyone, I couldn't expect that "anyone" would be interested in it (unless they were members of my family). Further, my attempts to distill so many years into a readable text revealed its inevitable limitations: "It's interesting . . . what's the point?" was sounded from sharp-eyed reviewers. These comments echoed years of conversations with colleagues across the nation regarding the CWC: it was amazing, sure, but it must have been an anomaly, an emergence of good fortune that had little relevancy beyond its local context. Typically, collegial interest waned when I could not provide instructions for, or a model of, how to get a community writing center started in other locales.

I started to ask myself just what message—or messages—did I want to get across with this book. I knew that the SLCC Community Writing Center was an important part of the history of the academic fields it belonged to, but how to articulate this? In a frustrated message to my chair, Stephen Ruffus, I wrote,

> There are so many different avenues into this work, it makes the mind swirl. . . . It brings together Freire, Gee, Street, Heath, Brandt, Flower, Shor, Rose, Cushman, Mathieu, Certeau, Goldblatt, Parks, and on and on. . . . For me, it boils down to the rhetoric of respect for the "wholeness" of a person or collection of people, [rather than] the way that education and academia in particular seem to view people as "not finished" or "lacking" or "in need."

I didn't know what to do.

Two kind people helped me to find my way out of this mess. First, Ellen Cushman, a reviewer of an earlier draft, provided me with encouragement and insight that directly led to what you are reading now. In her review, she suggested that I might be able to tap into "the thorny question of sustainability," because "[the CWC] helps us explore the longstanding question of where change takes place." I took that review to Ruffus, who suggested that I look into the literature of ecocomposition. Though I'd heard of this subfield of composition, I had not given it any thought because my work at the CWC didn't have anything to do with nature, nor preservation of natural spaces (save the occasional writing workshop we might have done in collaboration with environmental organizations).

Championed by Sidney I. Dobrin and Christian R. Weisser, ecocomposition seeks to further the postprocess movement in composition studies by turning to place/environment as a critical path of inquiry into the production and consumption of written discourse (6). Drawing on the interdisciplinary field of ecology and utilizing its epistemological processes, via method and metaphor, ecocomposition is often associated with environmental politics, yet it is not limited to the "green" movement. Rather, ecocomposition provides a lens into relationships, places, and systems that both affect and are affected by discourse. One focus of ecocomposition examines discursive ecology, which "see[s] writing as an ecological process, [and] explore[s] writing and writing processes as systems of interaction, economy, and interconnectedness" (116). Arguing that "very little of what we do now in composition studies is not ecological" (63), Dobrin, Weisser, and others emphasize the potential of ecocomposition to deepen our understanding of the forces that act on, and are changed by, writers interacting with one another through writing.

When I looked into it, I found that ecocomposition did indeed provide a means for me to examine the Community Writing Center in ways that felt familiar. I found metaphors that I had already been using: organism, environment, relationship, place, and the "retroactively labeled" concept of the "web" in Marilyn Cooper's "The Ecology of Writing" (Dobrin and Weisser 118).[2] Moreover, my own relationship with the CWC had been an organic one; I often thought of it as my "first child" and have gone through stages with the CWC that parallel those of a parent: gestation, labor, birth, nurturing, worrying, trusting, the happiness of seeing other people come to love it, followed by the satisfied—yet bittersweet—knowledge that it was time for me to leave so it could grow in new and different ways without me.[3]

In addition to the resonance of ecocomposition for me personally, its theories also provided a frame for a concept I'd been trying to build my inquiry around, one that arose from attempts to interpret a micro-change that countless people seemed to experience at the Community Writing Center. This individualized transformation tended to be marked by a specific "look" that crossed over the faces of people entering the CWC for the first time and learning about its programs. Typically accompanied by glancing around the center with what looked like confusion—but wasn't quite—this "look" became part of CWC lore, with writing assistants tallying how many times they'd witnessed (or provoked) it over the course of a day. While we all recognized it, we didn't understand what the "look" meant. It wasn't just about finding a new community resource, which might elicit excited or happy responses. Rather, it seemed to emerge from something found and lost at the same time.

Talking about it one day, Rachel Meads, who had worked at the CWC for nearly three years before entering a PhD program in radical education, introduced me to Elizabeth Ellsworth's research into *anomalous learning spaces,* which put "inside and outside into relation" with each other (*Places* 37). In such spaces, people encounter learning moments different from those they may move through in educational institutions. In anomalous learning spaces, people may experience their learning selves "in transition and in motion," sometimes unexpectedly, "towards previously unknown ways of thinking and being in the world" (16). Although such spaces may not be identified as educational environments, they "[put] inner thoughts, feelings, memories, fears, desires, and ideas in relation to outside others, events, history, culture, and socially constructed ideas" (37). These spaces, like the Vietnam Veterans Memorial on the National Mall or the Hirsoshima Peace Memorial Museum in

Japan, move participants through a "pedagogical pivot point," a moment when the learning self "comes into relation with the outside world and to the other selves who inhabit and create that world with us" (117). This moment of transformation is unmediated by a teacher or professor; instead, it is revealed by the learning self's sharp awareness of relationship.

Meads offered the insight that the "look" was the expression of moving through such a transition, pivoting through one's relationship with education and writing. She suggested that people came into the center thinking it was just a "front" for Salt Lake Community College; after a little conversation with a writing assistant, however, they "got to turn a little bit; they adjust how they've been interacting with writing." Encountering a possibility of writing and learning in a nonacademic space may have led to micro-changes of self and the self's relation to literacy. The relationship-based theories of ecocomposition added to the frame I was constructing from Ellsworth's (*Places*) pivot metaphor in their focus on how organisms (writers) interact with their environments. When people entered the CWC's discursive space, the relationship between self and writing was often distinctly separate—many people never imagined they could be considered a "writer." However, the "look" suggested a blurring of this division, an integration of self and writing—perhaps an emergence of a writing self.

Correspondingly, Ellsworth's description of moving through a pedagogical pivot point brought to mind Marilyn Cooper's "web." According to Cooper, an ecological model of writing suggests a web in which "anything that affects one strand of the web vibrates throughout the whole" (370). To use this metaphor to examine change, however, I think we need to look not at the strands but at the connective spaces (the pivot points) where they meet: the intersections and "crossroads" that require change. Each of these points on a web calls forth possibilities: Which direction do I turn? What might happen if I do? What choices do I have? These points require that decisions be made; we cannot stay at an intersection forever.

With decisions come loss, perhaps very small, sometimes great—options that were open close, and perhaps others open. Thus, moving through a web's intersections is commonly marked by what Ellsworth describes as a vulnerability that emerges when the "inside" self relates to the world outside it (*Places*). She argues that pivot points are not the experience of comprehending new knowledge necessary to meet educational or professional requirements, such as finally understanding how a particular mathematical concept works or doing well on an exam. These moments of accomplishment are framed by "satisfaction, relief, [or] triumph upon arriving at the end of a process and grasping . . . the 'right' answer" (16). Rather, moving through a pedagogical pivot point is often an unexpected transition and looks like "someone who is in the process of losing something of who she thought she was . . . upon encountering something outside herself and her own ways of thinking" (16). Similarly, the points on a web are spaces of transition, of decision, of change—they combine possibility and loss. The "look" that punctuated the Community Writing Center's space may have been the expression of this moment: the loss of one's current sense of self and the onset of another.

Lest it appear that I am interested only in the change that community members experienced at the Community Writing Center, let me emphasize that the people who worked there—the staff and I—experienced change as well, as will be apparent in the chapters that follow. For now, however, let me provide a small sample of how my own relationship to the CWC, and to teaching, was in continual motion, and in some ways still is, now three years after leaving the center. Specifically, I'd like to illustrate how intersections inherently precede change, the moments when we must make a decision to follow one strand of the web or another. One particular junction that forever altered how I related to literacy education appeared when I was working with an early CWC writing group. This was only my second experience in facilitating writing partnerships with a nonprofit organization; I was still new at this kind of work. In this particular partnership, I was repeating a curriculum that explored themes of self and community, a curriculum I had used only once before with another organization. In the third of eight scheduled meetings, the participants asked me why I expected them to write about themselves in personal ways yet didn't offer to write about myself. Their question threw me because I was used to the safe space that existed for me as a teacher in a college environ-ment. Students usually did what I asked them to; however, this group of "not students" put their pens down and said they wouldn't write until I agreed to expose myself just as much as I was asking of them. At that moment, I found myself at a crossroads; the way I turned would determine my relationship with these writers and with myself.

I agreed to write with them, and entered into a space I had not experienced before in a teaching situation, even when I'd written along with composition students. In such classroom environments, I knew I could write more sophisticated essays than the students could; therefore, the risk I took in doing so was minimal. When I wrote about myself and my communities, however, and then shared my writing with a public audience, I felt scared and exposed. I had lost the protective (and protected) space of the academy. At the same time, I had discovered something important about how I would try to relate with community partners and individuals, and by extension, how the Community Writing Center would too—I would prioritize *respect* for (though, importantly, not coddle or feel sorry for) human vulnerability and would ask someone to risk only what I was willing to risk myself.

Thus, to corral the past decade of my work with the SLCC Community Writing Center into something meaningful for com-positionists, writing center workers, and community literacy ac-tivist-scholars, I turn to metaphors in ecocomposition. I want to be clear, however, that I do not see my work as necessarily con-tributing to ecocomposition theory; rather, I use its discourse to recognize change and how such insights shaped why the SLCC Community Writing Center emerged, how it (and the people in-volved with it) transformed, and how it was sustained over so many years. This inquiry is not merely local. The CWC has long existed at the intersections (and outermost strands) of rhetoric, composi-tion, writing center, and community literacy studies, and, as such, its work can contribute to recognizing—rather than defining— change within progressive educational practices, and how flexibility and uncertainty can play meaningful roles in building sustainable partnerships. Further, this investigation reveals a way of cultivating relationships through a rhetoric of respect (which I explicate in the second chapter), a rhetoric that provided the seeds for the SLCC Community Writing Center and subsequently grew it into a thriving, yet disruptive, institution.

To provide a shared understanding of what the center was, in the first chapter, "Recognizing the SLCC Community Writing Center," I present the CWC as a specific locale and set of programs—its "what," "who," and "where"—that existed inside of the larger environment of community writing programs (academic and nonacademic) and within Salt Lake City and Salt Lake Community College. After laying this groundwork, I move into Chapter 2, "Evolving a Discursive Ecology: A Rhetoric of Respect," which describes the ideological metaphor that grounded the relationships internal to the CWC and in interaction with individuals and organizations. This chapter follows a narrative path from the development of my own understanding of what type of educational environment I wished to participate in through the negotiation of ideology and relationship with others as the Community Writing Center transformed from ideas into an actual project and space. The next chapter, "Transforming Energy in Pursuit of Uncertainty," looks at how a rhetoric of respect influenced change in the Community Writing Center within the collective groups of students and faculty who worked there. Specifically, I inquire into disruptions of academic notions of expertise that took place in the collaborative environment of the CWC, as well as the contribution that ease with uncertainty made toward the center's sustainability. In the fourth chapter, "Shifting Relations, Transforming Expectations," I map external relationships with the CWC to trace how we moved from a "liberatory" sense of the center as a site of empowerment or change-making into a rhetoric of respect for the ability of individuals to exercise agency over their textual production in ways they deemed most appropriate. Finally, in Chapter 5, "Engaging Place: Acclimation and Disruption," I return to ecocomposition's assertion of place as a critical path of inquiry and negotiate the tensions of sustainability and disturbance, of institutional power and resistance.

ACKNOWLEDGMENTS

THERE ARE MANY PEOPLE LIVING IN THE STORIES of this book and many more who contributed to the life of the SLCC Community Writing Center (CWC). While I couldn't work as many of their voices into these pages as I had hoped to, I want to recognize their impact on the CWC and, subsequently, this book's development.

First of all, I want to thank Salt Lake Community College for taking a risk on such a center, especially David Richardson, Geoffrey Brugger, Helen Cox, John McCormick, and President Cynthia Bioteau. Without these passionate administrators, the CWC never would have seen the light of day, much less been sustained for more than a decade. Next, I want to thank the entire SLCC English department, whose support for the CWC—and for me as their colleague—has been steadfast. I want to recognize Stephen Ruffus, cofounder of the CWC, in particular. Stephen constantly encouraged me in my leadership of the CWC and advocated fiercely for the center itself. His belief in what we were doing kept me going when things seemed unfeasible or futile. I also want to recognize Clint Gardner, who modeled excellence in writing center leadership. He answered every call for help or guidance that I sent his way, no matter how big or small, from the first inklings of the CWC to my last day as director. His genuine enthusiasm for the Student Writing Center's relationship with the Community Writing Center continues to inspire me. Finally, I want to thank Melissa Helquist and Andrea Malouf for their intellect, drive, and dedication as assistant directors. They both accomplished so much with the limited time and resources they had.

This book would not have been possible without the phenomenally unwavering commitment to the SLCC Community Writing Center brought each day by the writing assistants. I am forever thankful to each one of these students and community members and deeply value the opportunity to work alongside them—some for several months, some for several years. I honor them in chronological order of their work at the CWC: Catherine Lund, Kendra (Warren) Thompson, Sara Gunderson, Stephanie McKee, Michelle Kirkwood, Dennis Farrell, Shon Harper, Adrianna Reitenbach, Joanna Sewall, Scott Duran, Hazel Roehrig, Tina Groves, Shelly Barron, Tania Paxton, Maria Jaramillo, Lyndsey Scull, Susan Cummings, Kim Burgess, Elizabeth Coleman, Adam Walden, Adam Bowles, Rachel Meads, Jona Gerlach, Nina Liggett, Jeremy Remy, Chanel Earl, Von Jones, Christina Smith, Shannon Bell, Quintin Graves, Robbi Poulson, Dave Hansen, Suzy Gehring, Ken Simin, Alisabeth McQueen, and David Alder. Additionally, I want to thank my father, Phil Rousculp, for numerous conversations that helped me figure out how to develop respectful, supportive, and productive relationships with the writing assistants.

Many more people from the college and the Salt Lake community gave of their time, energy, and intellect to make the Community Writing Center a reality. I can't possibly name everyone, but several need to be recognized here: Susan Miller, Stephen Goldsmith, Jackie Skibine, Karen Hoffman, Lou Ann Olsen, Anne Chapman, David Gravelle, John Wilkes, Lou Borgenicht, Betsy Ward, David Bastian, Colleen McLaughlin, Cynthia Talbot-Holz, Ron Christiansen, Lisa Bickmore, Lynn Kilpatrick, Stephanie Maenhardt, Dean Huber, Betty Starks, Christopher LeCluyse, Sundy Watanabe, Shauna Bona, Jennifer Ritter, Ann Holman, Ken Verdoia, Christine Young, Jamie McBeth-Smith, Gail Jessen, Jennifer Saunders, Deborah Young, Elisa Stone, Richard Scott, Nancy Tessman, Jim Dykman, Kay Robinson, Rosanita Cespedes, Maureen Mathison, Cheryl Shurtleff, and Beth Elder.

Founding and directing a community writing center is one thing; writing a book about it is something entirely different. The former is realized through constant exchange, collaboration, and shared experience. The other requires solitary spaces to think, to shape, to draft. Yet this book is also a product of collaborating rather than going it alone. First, I must mention again Stephen Ruffus, who simply assumed I would write this book and gave me no option to consider otherwise. Next, I want to thank my community literacy and writing colleagues (and exemplars) Eli Golblatt, Linda Flower, Stephen Parks, Paula Mathieu, Tobi Jacobi, Thomas Ferrel, Eliana Schoenberg, Melissa Tedrowe, Michelle Hall Kells, and Julie Wilson. Their continual reminders that they wanted to read about the SLCC Community Writing Center kept me on a purposeful path.

The many and varied readers of this manuscript gave me honest and unflinching feedback, without which this book would still be a tangled mess. I thank my mother, Beverly Rousculp, who read through each page of an earlier draft, the one that I intended to reach a nonacademic audience. She alerted me to where my writing became muddy and uninteresting and where it conveyed clarity and relevance. Reviewers Ellen Cushman and Mary Soliday took that draft and urged me to reshape it into what it has become. At the time, their requests seemed insurmountable, but they were spot-on in their sharp insights. I am grateful for their tough and encouraging guidance. Series Editor Victor Villanueva saw the potential in this book; his support for it and for me has warmed my spirit. Allison Fernley of the SLCC English department graciously read my revision, examining its theoretical and stylistic cohesion, as well as its relevance to the field of composition beyond community literacy studies. Her responses were both sweeping and detailed, an invaluable combination from an exceptional reviewer. Thank you also to Bonny Graham, Kim Black, and Robin Gosser, whose editing and organizing dexterities led this project through its conclusion.

Finally, my greatest thanks and appreciation go to my husband, Chris Lippard. Not only did he read and respond to each version of this book project, but he also constantly supported and loved me throughout my relationship with the SLCC Community Writing Center. He was there from the beginning, through every drama and failure, every achievement and success, and was waiting for me at the end. Without him, neither the CWC nor this book would have been possible. I remain ever grateful to him.

1

Recognizing the SLCC Community Writing Center

"You mean I can come here to write?"
"Yep."
"And I don't have to be a student?"
"Nope."
"I can write what I want? And someone will help me?"
"Yep."
"Yeah, well, what does it cost?"
"Nothing."
"Is this for real?"
"Sure is."
"I've always wanted to be a writer."
"You already are."

IN HIS BOOK *BECAUSE WE LIVE HERE: Sponsoring Literacy beyond the College Curriculum*, Eli Goldblatt asserts the relevance of local context to literacy: "If one pursues a vision of writing or literacy instruction that goes beyond the campus, indeed beyond the curriculum, there is all the more reason to understand that program in its very specific locale" (9). Therefore, I present the Salt Lake Community College (SLCC) Community Writing Center (CWC) in its locale—a specific site, set of programs, and people. Before doing so, however, it is important to recognize that the CWC existed within a myriad of programs dedicated to writing with the community. My use of the word *with* is intentional and references Thomas Deans's classification of academy–community engagement projects into "writing *about*, writing *for*, and writing *with*" the community. In such programs, community members are not primarily objects of research or recipients of textual or literacy services; rather, they participate in relationships within writing.

There are many such efforts, ranging from activist teachers/ scholars and writing centers collaborating with communities to nonprofit organizations targeting specific audiences or focusing on specific genres of writing. Some are large and complex while others are local and temporary. The number of colleges and universities working with their surrounding communities has increased exponentially over the last two decades, particularly through service-learning initiatives. This community writing movement has been explored by many scholars, including Paula Mathieu in *Tactics of Hope: The Public Turn in English Composition*, Elenore Long in *Community Literacy and the Rhetoric of Local Publics*, and Thomas Deans, Barbara Roswell, and Adrian Wurr in their edited collection, *Writing and Community Engagement: A Critical Sourcebook*. Further, there are thousands of community writing projects and programs that have no relationship to academic institutions: ad hoc writing groups, nonprofit writing organizations, community publishing programs, and more. Clearly, there are more community-based writing efforts going on than can be represented here. Still, to understand the specific manifestation of "writing *with*" that the SLCC Community Writing Center cultivated, it is useful to situate the CWC within a small constellation of particularly relevant community writing programs.

To begin, the Community Literacy Center (CLC), a collaboration between the National Center for the Study of Writing and Literacy at Carnegie Mellon University (CMU) and the Community House in Pittsburgh, has been noted as an archetypal "writing with" partnership.[1] Led by Wayne C. Peck, Linda Flower, and Lorraine Higgins, the CLC sought "to reinvent [a] tradition of community and university interaction . . . with attention centered on collaborative problem solving and the appreciation of multiple kinds of expertise" (203). Together, CMU faculty and graduate students worked with Community House members to develop partnerships that paired Pittsburgh youth and CMU students in writing and publishing projects. Other projects gathered large groups of stakeholders in *problem-solving dialogues* that used *rivaling* methods to get at the *story behind the story* of a civic dilemma in order to produce alternative solutions for change.[2] As we developed the Community Writing Center, we looked to the CLC's programs, intentions, and organizational structures for guidance and inspiration.

Another early iteration of academy–community collaboration we drew from was the Institute for the Study of Literature, Literacy, and Culture (ISLLC) at Temple University in Philadelphia. Headed by Stephen Parks and Eli Goldblatt, the ISLLC was "devoted to furthering interdisciplinary studies both within and beyond the confines of the University" and produced *Open City: A Journal of Community Arts and Culture,* which published writing from Philadelphia neighborhoods. The ISLLC evolved into the New City Community Press, a continuing collaboration that "provide[s] opportunities for local communities to represent themselves by telling their stories in their own words" ("Institute").[3]

Many notable programs have connected colleges and universities with their communities. The Digital Underground Storytelling for Youth (DUSTY) is "a collaboration between the University of California, Berkeley's Graduate School of Education and West Oakland's Prescott-Joseph Center for Community Enhancement" that "aims to help bridge the 'digital divide' and boost the ability of children and adults in the underserved community to read and write through the use of images, sound and text" (Maclay). The mission of Colorado State University's Community Literacy Center is to "create alternative literacy opportunities in order to educate and empower underserved populations (e.g., incarcerated juveniles and adults, adult learners, women, at-risk youth, English Language Learners) and to support university–community literacy outreach programs" (*Community*). Michelle Hall Kells, from the University of New Mexico (UNM), spearheaded the development of a Writing Across Communities Alliance project that "[comprises] students, faculty, and community members committed to the importance of writing and literacy across the campus and within the greater community" (*Writing*). In 2011, graduate students at UNM launched the ABQ Community Writing Center, and more recently, Auburn

University started up its own CWC. Scores of academy–community writing projects exist, as does the activist and engaged scholarship of individual researchers, including Linda Adler-Kassner, Ellen Cushman, Jeffrey T. Grabill, Diana George, Michael T. Moore, and others.[4]

Within higher education, writing centers also develop relationships with their surrounding communities. The University of Wisconsin–Madison has sponsored, with grant support, a long-standing Community Writing Assistance program in downtown Madison libraries, where UW–Madison students tutor community members in writing (Doggart, Tedrowe, and Viera).[5] Similarly, the University of Iowa Writing Center sponsors the Library Community Writing Center at the Iowa City Public Library, with UI students serving as tutors. At the University of North Carolina–Chapel Hill, the Writing Center partnered with the Durham County Library to offer the Write On! Community Writing Center, which sponsors writing workshops for local teenagers.[6] The Ohio State University's Center for the Study and Teaching of Writing has long sponsored substantial outreach programs, including tutoring elementary students in reading and writing, engaging high school students in intensive weeklong workshops, and training K–12 teachers on new writing technologies. More and more writing centers are engaging with their communities, from large centers like the one at Purdue University (Bergmann) to smaller ones such as the Casper College Writing Center in Wyoming (G. Cooper).[7]

Lest I create the impression that the academy sponsors the lion's share of such community writing programs, let me turn quickly to a selection of community-based writing programs (which does not include the thousands of programs that identify themselves as "literacy centers" with missions primarily based on reading acquisition). As the SLCC Community Writing Center developed its community writing group and publication program, the DiverseCity Writing Series, we turned to the Write Around Portland program in Oregon and the Neighborhood Writing Alliance in Chicago for guidance. Both of these programs facilitate writing group and publication projects to promote the production and consumption of the multiplicity of voices in their communities. Write Around Portland partners with local organizations in a series of writing workshops,[8] while the Neighborhood Writing Alliance holds year-round writing group meetings in community centers and libraries around the city.[9] Both programs publish anthologies of writing on a regular basis.

Other nonprofit community writing programs also promote publication as a part of their missions.[10] The Neighborhood Story Project (NSP) in New Orleans identifies itself as a "bookmaking project" that "works with writers in neighborhoods around New Orleans to write books about their communities" (*Neighborhood*). The NSP, which partners with the University of New Orleans, has published nearly twenty books written by local residents. Additionally, the New York Writers Coalition, Inc. "provides free creative writing workshops throughout New York City for people from groups that have been historically deprived of voice in our society" ("New York"), publishes participants' writing, and stages public reading events. Also in New York City, Girls Write Now combines writing instruction and mentoring to "provide guidance, support, and opportunities for at-risk and underserved teenage girls" ("Girls").

Another community writing program that came together at the same time as the CWC was the phenomenally successful "826" writing program, which began in San Francisco in a storefront on Valencia Street (hence the first center's name: 826 Valencia). Founded by author Dave Eggers and educator Nínive Calegari in 2002, and fronted by a whimsical "pirate supply" shop, 826 Valencia provides an extensive range of programs, including free tutoring to youth ages six to eighteen, writing workshops for youth and adults, writing assistance to public school teachers, and a series of publications. The success of the 826 movement is remarkable, with chapters in New York City, Chicago, Los Angeles, Seattle, Ann Arbor (Michigan), and Boston, as well as many other centers that have based themselves on the 826 model in cities across the nation (*826national.org*).

The SLCC Community Writing Center shared much with these

programs. Like them and all human-based endeavors, the CWC existed like a living organism, mutating and adapting to specific environments and discovering certain "ranges of tolerance"—the limits of its survivability—which it had to retreat from or respond to by revising itself. The CWC's particular intentions, resources, relationships, and sustainability, however, distinguish it in ways that lie at the heart of its value to progressive and activist educators. This book attempts to uncover that value. Before doing so, however, it is important first to recognize the SLCC Community Writing Center as a distinct entity within the broad scope of community-based writing programs—to understand its "what," "who," and "where," before moving into the "why" and "how" of inquiry.

RECOGNIZING THE "WHAT"

Opening in the fall of 2001, the SLCC Community Writing Center was dedicated to providing flexible and innovative writing and literacy opportunities for people living in the Salt Lake metropolitan area. Funded by Salt Lake Community College yet located off-campus—first in a low-income, multi-use neighborhood development (the Artspace Bridge Projects) near the city's homeless services district, and later on the public plaza of the Salt Lake City Library's Main Branch—the CWC was founded with the mission to support, motivate, and educate people of all abilities and educational backgrounds who wanted to use writing for practical needs, civic engagement, and personal expression. In both locations, the center was industrially designed with concrete floors, exposed heating-and-cooling systems, and cavernous spaces. The walls were covered with shelves of books and CWC publications, pictures of CWC events, and poster-sized framed selections of CWC writers' work. A small "classroom" formed the only closed-off space in both locations, the rest open and unbounded by walls or doors. There were no offices at the CWC—the director, associate director, and writing assistants worked at desks and round tables scattered around the center.

In "An Ideal Writing Center: Re-Imagining Space and Design," Hadfield, Kinkead, Peterson, Ray, and Preston visualize a writing center with similar open space, yet also include private rooms for tutoring sessions and private offices for directors' "confidential conversations regarding the administration of the center" (173). I had been offered a director's office in both of the CWC's designs but turned it down so as to not section myself off physically or symbolically from the writing assistants or writers with whom I was sharing the space. Though I typically sat at a specific desk, it was a transitory workspace, not a territory marked as mine only; others used it when I was not there or if I was working elsewhere. The center's intentional arrangement diffused the power that my position held over the writing assistants, forced interaction between everyone in the center, and generated its fair share of chaos, as the interaction of many bodies and opinions in one small space is certain to do. When circumstances required privacy, discussions took place outside on the plaza, in the library, or in the CWC's classroom, where the thin walls encouraged people to stay calm and respectful in stressful situations. Inside the CWC's space (at both locations), noise dominated: conversations constantly crossed over one another, interrupting intense concentration and generating unexpected ideas.[11]

Between 2001 and 2010, the Community Writing Center housed four main programs that engaged with people in one-on-one, small-group, large-group, and institutional partnerships. During that time, about 5,000 people and more than 130 organizations worked with the CWC in its two locations, as well as in city and county libraries, nonprofit organizations, government agencies, public schools, community centers, and, occasionally, outside in city parks and festivals.

Writing Coaching

Adjivah,[12] a Bosnian woman living in Salt Lake City on her own,[13] became a part of the Community Writing Center for more than two years. While her young son played in the CWC's "Children's Corner," reading books and playing with puzzles, Adjivah worked with writing coaches on reading, writing, and speaking activities. She was initially drawn to the center to improve her pronunciation of written English because she worked in a day care center and was embarrassed when she made mistakes while reading out loud, especially when the children corrected her. Over time her confidence grew, and she "pivoted" in her sense of herself as a user of language. Rather than continuing to chase after perfect pronunciation, she let go of embarrassment over mistakes to make room for her emerging identity as a writer. Beginning with short sentences, Adjivah collaborated with writing coaches on a nearly weekly basis, eventually writing the story of how she came from Bosnia to the United States. She also began volunteering for the center as she wrote, contributing her time and abilities to type up handwritten submissions to CWC publications.

The CWC's Writing Coaching program, offered at the CWC and at libraries and community centers across the city, resembled tutoring, advising, or consulting in student writing centers on college campuses and high schools. Though we were sensitive to the fact that "the act of naming constitutes a place as having particular boundaries, particular functions, and particular identities" (Dobrin and Weisser 51), we first clumsily called this program Individual Writing Assistance. In our attempt to avoid student–tutor discourses that might have dissuaded people from coming to the center, we practically erased the human connection inherent in sharing writing with someone else. Eventually, in response to community focus groups, the name was changed to Writing Coaching. The exchange was familiar to that in student writing centers: two people coming together—one, a writer,[14] seeking advice, feedback, assistance, and/or direction, the second engaging through interested and skilled reading, listening, and conversation. At the CWC, writing coaches—both staff and volunteers—worked with people on any kind of writing, sometimes for a single session, sometimes for more than a year.

Through Writing Coaching, some writers, like Adjivah, experienced a change in their self-perception from "nonwriter" to "writer," or from "needing help" to "capable." Other times, changes reached beyond the individual writer into the larger web of the community. Long-time writing assistant Shannon Bell worked over the course of a month with a man named Roger who was struggling with a government work-training program. He wanted to become a barber for people with Afro-textured hair and was seeking funding for professional training. Unfortunately, the program repeatedly rejected his request because barbering was not considered a job with a guaranteed income. He was told to seek training in another area, but because he had a felony criminal record, Roger believed he would need to be his own boss, that no one would hire someone with a past like his. Besides, Salt Lake City's limited number of barbershops catering to African and African American clientele convinced Roger there was money to be made. Together, Roger and Shannon worked on a letter asking the agency to reconsider the program's policy. Although Roger wanted to give up, he continued to return to the CWC over the course of several weeks. About a month after their last coaching session, Roger came back to tell Shannon that the agency had agreed with him, would pay for his training, and would also be changing their policy about certain jobs needing guaranteed incomes.

Writing Workshops

When the CWC opened, we assumed that we would be swamped with writers requesting coaching; student writing centers always are, so that was undoubtedly going to be the case at a writing center available to the entire community. That didn't happen. The myth of the "solitary genius writer" that discourages students from initially visiting on-campus writing centers, along with the fear of sharing writing with complete strangers, also applied to nonstudent populations—perhaps even more so. For several years, we spent more time trying to explain what writing coaching was than actually doing it.

Workshops, however, were a different story. During our first year, we persistently sought input from the public regarding what they wanted from a community writing center. Writing workshops topped the list of requests, but we had no budget to pay workshop facilitators and we didn't want to create a barrier by charging high fees. (A few years later, we began charging a small "commitment" fee, which we waived for financial need—a very informal process of simply approving any request made for it.) Even though I could teach an occasional workshop, the demand far outstripped what I could do alone, and the five part-time CWC writing assistants were community college students trained only to work one on one with writers. After about six months of watching requests pile up, Stephanie McKee, an energetic writing assistant, announced that she wanted to teach a workshop on journaling. Although the idea of a student teaching a public workshop felt a bit risky to me, her coaching training wasn't being put to use because no one was coming in for it. If she was willing to try something new, I didn't want to stop her. Together, we designed a two-hour "Introduction to Journaling" workshop. McKee posted signs around the area announcing the workshop, and on a Saturday afternoon, eight community members showed up to write. This small mutation, this slight pivot in how writing assistants saw themselves at the Community Writing Center, completely changed the center's scope and future. McKee's declaration of what a writing assistant could do rippled through the rest of the student employees, and they eagerly turned toward defining what a writing assistant was themselves. Collaboratively, we (and later, they) designed workshop curricula for more journaling, poetry writing, résumé writing, getting through writer's block, creating newsletters, grant writing, fiction writing, and more. The center was unruly as we tried to respond quickly to requests that flooded in, turning out workshops within a week or two. As curricula began filling up our paper files and electronic folders, we started to schedule workshop "seasons" to meet institutional marketing deadlines. In an effort to organize files for the new director upon my departure from the CWC in 2010, I scrolled through more than 100 different types of workshops designed for vastly different audiences, nearly all of them facilitated by undergraduate student writing assistants.

The DiverseCity Writing Series
Before the CWC was a place, there was the DiverseCity Writing Series (DWS), established in the fall of 2000. In collaboration with two work-study students at SLCC and facilitated out of my faculty

office, we started with a small, eight-week writing group workshop with a single nonprofit partner. From there, the DWS grew into a year-round program, with more than a dozen different writing groups and the regular production of an anthology, *sine cera*.[15] The DWS's purposes were to complicate the notion of "diversity" beyond that of ethnicity or race (most often at the forefront of discussions on diversity) and to bridge multiple differences (class, age, education, sexual orientation, belief, and experience) that lead to alienation.

In the pilot project, the DWS partnered with Dignity for Women, a nonprofit organization advocating for low-income women. Funded by a small grant from the Utah Humanities Council, the project worked with eight women for two months, writing on themes of self and community, and resulted in a zine publication and public reading event. Working with partners continued after the Community Writing Center opened to the public. Three more times the CWC partnered with a single organization through the DiverseCity Writing Series—a homeless shelter (whose writers, I mentioned earlier, dared me to write along with them), a senior center, and a cancer support center. After the fourth DWS partnership, we realized that we wanted to expand the DWS program into one with multiple partners that met year-round. Another writing assistant, Sara Gunderson, took charge. After researching community publication programs around the nation, Gunderson found Write Around Portland in Oregon and the Neighborhood Writing Alliance in Chicago. Using ideas from each and supported by a small SLCC grant, we evolved the DWS into a program that produced twelve anthologies of community writing over seven years.[16]

Writing Partners

The least well-defined program at the Community Writing Center, demarcated by relationship rather than specific activity, the Writing Partners program consisted of collaborations between the CWC and organizations, institutions, and agencies on a wide variety of projects and programs. Adhering to the principle that the CWC "do[es] not duplicate already existing writing services or programs; rather, the CWC coordinates with other organizations to mutual

mutual benefit

benefit" (see Appendix A), we collaborated with organizations in various configurations and for various purposes.

In early Writing Partners development, its collaborations were imagined to be long term as a way to create sustainable change in the capacities of the partner organization. Motivated by Ellen Cushman's call for faculty to develop prolonged and layered relationships with partner organizations ("Sustainable"), we declared that the CWC would partner with an organization for six months to a year, exploring together how writing might improve conditions for their staff, volunteers, and/or clients. However, similar to our assumptions about the Writing Coaching program, our sense of the Partners program proved to be quite wrong. (In Chapter 4, I show just how wrong we were.)

It's not possible to create a full picture of the CWC's many partnerships, but a sampling can reveal their range. Partners included nonprofit organizations, governmental agencies, and, occasionally, for-profit organizations (which generated a little income to support programming). Sometimes partners had specific tasks they wanted the CWC to fulfill. For example, a center supporting survivors of sexual violence wanted to become more politically active and enlisted the CWC to facilitate an activist writing workshop for their board members. In another instance, a nonprofit umbrella group advocating for in-home child care providers (mostly stay-at-home mothers trying to make ends meet by caring for others' children) asked the CWC to provide instruction so the providers could respond successfully to short essay sections newly added to state certification applications.

Other partnerships became driven by relationship rather than outcome. A nonprofit organization supporting homeless youth asked the CWC to facilitate the production of writing for an in-house zine, which quickly became secondary to the importance of the CWC providing a mentor to ensure that the youth could participate (if they chose to) in reliable, ongoing writing group meetings each week in their office space. Another partnership, this one with a county-wide mental health agency, began with a two-month writing workshop—again predicated on publishing a zine—that soon became part of the agency's ongoing courses available to day treatment clients. While social workers collaborated with CWC writing assistants to develop a specific curriculum, week after week most of the agency's clients simply wrote what they wanted. The partnership shifted into providing the experience of writing with others, rather than producing texts for posterity or consumption.

Some partnerships became multifaceted, as with the Salt Lake City Library, our neighbor and landlord at the CWC's second location. Initially, partnerships with the library were short term, responding to their specific requests, such as résumé writing workshops for employment events or contributions to annual literary celebrations. In 2009 this partnership formalized into a package of services in exchange for rent reduction. One part of the package was a monthly series of Writing for Change events, in which library patrons were introduced to strategies for writing to their political representatives. Though they started slowly, these events grew to be anticipated and pulled in respected community activists to encourage community members to write for change.

events

RECOGNIZING THE "WHO"

The Writers

In the few months before the CWC opened in October 2001, while Clint Gardner (coordinator of the SLCC Student Writing Center) and I were training the brand-new group of student writing assistants, everyone decided that people who participated in CWC programs would be named "writers." We revisited this decision several times over the years and always returned to *writers* as the most appropriate term. When people participated in CWC programs, they wrote. A person who writes is a writer, although some clients found being called a "writer" temporarily unsettling—something reserved only for published authors or people who earned a living by writing. Over time, however, most CWC writers adapted to seeing themselves as such and snapped up CWC T-shirts—emblazoned with "I Write Stuff . . ." on the front and ". . . with the SLCC Community Writing Center" on the back—faster than we could keep them in stock.

T-shirts (publicity)

It's hard to classify CWC writers because our ability (and desire) to track demographic information varied based on location: at the CWC itself, we registered people and asked for information, but off-site projects were less amenable to data collection. Registration requires a person to enter into a bureaucratic relationship with an institution; when someone came to the CWC, it seemed acceptable to ask for this information in exchange for participation in that space. But when an individual wanted to join a CWC writing group held in a bookstore or community center, the question of who "owned" that environment complicated the idea of registration. Further, we were concerned that a registration requirement (including providing demographic information) would hinder public participation in events such as writing letters to members of the Utah legislature or contributing to a New Year's Eve public poetry event. In the former, doing so might have erected a discursive barrier to a basic civic right; in the latter, filling out paperwork certainly would have dampened the spontaneity of a celebratory moment. In cases such as these, we counted writers but let demographics fall by the wayside. Even so, we were able to collect enough information to provide a general cumulative description of writers who established relationships with the CWC between 2001 and 2010.

On average, between 350 and 400 people registered with the CWC each year, and it is safe to say that another 300 distinct individuals participated in CWC writing partnerships or writing groups annually. (This does not include the hundreds of people who participated in community writing events—such as the CWC literary arts programming at the Utah Arts Festival—each year since 2005.) Many writers developed extended relationships with the CWC as well, returning for multiple writing coaching sessions, participating in one or more DWS groups, or coming back for new and different writing workshops.

Ethnically, slightly less than 30 percent of CWC writers identified themselves as persons of color, exceeding the percentage of persons of color living in Salt Lake County (the college's service area). Economically, CWC writers were less well-off than the average resident of Salt Lake County, where the 2010 child poverty rate was 12.5 percent (a $23,000 annual household income for a family of four) ("Poverty Rate"). Although the CWC did not ask for the number of people living in a household, we did ask for annual household income, and more than 43 percent of CWC writers were from households making less than $20,000 a year. Only 18 percent of CWC writers reported incomes higher than the Salt Lake County median of $59,000 ("Salt Lake County").

Within the web of adult literacy education options that existed in Salt Lake City when we were developing the CWC, we found a niche for the CWC's development: "The CWC aims to fill the 'gap' in our system: individuals who can read and write, but don't feel able to move freely to new writing/reading situations" (Rousculp, "SLCC"). Between 2001 and 2010, the educational demographics of CWC writers reflected this goal. Only 3 percent of CWC writers had not completed a high school degree, while just over 35 percent had earned a diploma or GED, 44 percent had their associate or bachelor's degree, and 13 percent held master's or doctorate degrees. CWC writers would be considered educated (or literate) by most quantitative standards, but they still sought to improve their writing abilities.[17]

The Staff

An important observation about the Community Writing Center's staff is that each person worked in multiple spaces: the director and the assistant director (a position created in 2006) were also SLCC faculty,[18] and the writing assistants were full-time students at Salt Lake Community College (SLCC), the University of Utah (U of U), or Westminster College. These conditions may not seem ideal to support a wide-ranging center, given that writing assistants worked only fifteen to twenty-five hours a week and the directors had teaching and college obligations to meet as well. Nonetheless, the interconnectedness and distinction of these responsibilities beyond the CWC, all based in learning environments, grounded the center's educational focus, which could easily have mutated into a service-based or "writing salon" approach to working with the community. When nonstudents were (very occasionally) hired as writing assistants, they typically had trouble adapting to the CWC's educational environment, as most were drawn to the center either to "serve the less fortunate" or to fulfill a romantic notion of "being paid to be a writer." It typically took a few months for nonstudent writing assistants to realize that neither of these missions would be fulfilled at the CWC, at which point most decided to move on.

While I directed the CWC, the college made a substantial financial commitment to the center, funding its rent, writing assistant wages, and reassigned time for faculty. It was difficult, however, to secure additional funding to cover the rapid growth of the center's programs as other college departments and programs competed for resources as well. With programs growing but not funding for resources, writing assistants worked very hard and were committed to the CWC far beyond what one would anticipate from employees making $10.00 an hour. Their identities evolved along with the CWC, they co-owned the programs that we developed together, and they fought tenaciously to make them work. Writing assistants advocated bringing the public into the center and pushed me to develop a volunteer program to support the CWC's growth. Colleagues in the nonprofit world had cautioned me about taking on volunteers with such limited infrastructure. Nonetheless, two particular writing assistants, Tina Groves and Joanna Sewall, were determined to create a volunteer program, and thankfully they did, for without the more than 250 volunteers who contributed their time to the CWC over the years, the DiverseCity Writing Series and off-site Writing Coaching programs would not have been possible. Volunteers also occasionally facilitated writing workshops or represented the CWC in partnerships. Additionally, academic and community volunteers served on the original CWC steering committee and subsequently constituted the advisory committees: the Academic Advisory Committee (AAC) and the Community Advisory Committee (CAC).[19]

RECOGNIZING THE "WHERE"

Though the SLCC Community Writing Center was its own specific environment, it was, of course, located within larger ecosystems:

Salt Lake City and Salt Lake Community College. As I describe these two much larger and more complex locales, I am reminded that this inquiry reflects my perspective. There are more than two million people living in the urban corridor, known as the Wasatch Front, in which Salt Lake City is located. As a transplant to the area nearly two decades ago for a faculty position at SLCC, my relationship with the city is quite different from that of people who have lived here longer and whose roots are in this land—and from that of more recent arrivals. Nevertheless, my interpretations of these environments inform my inquiry, and therefore, while not objectively reliable in any way, are important to recognizing the SLCC Community Writing Center within them.

Nestled between two mountain ranges that rise more than 5,000 feet above the valley floor (an ancient lake bed) to the east and west and two smaller ranges to the north and south, Salt Lake City, the capital of the State of Utah, is an urban area of slightly more than 100 square miles with a population of 187,000. (Salt Lake County expands to fill the valley and is home to just over a million people ["Salt Lake County"].) Salt Lake City (aka "Salt Lake" or "SLC") is the economic and political center of Utah. The city, founded within the territory of the Northwestern Shoshone Tribe, was settled in 1847 by the Church of Jesus Christ of Latter Day Saints (also known as "Mormon" or "LDS") whose members traveled beyond the boundaries of the United States to seek safe haven from religious persecution. (At the time, the settlement was part of Mexico; it became US territory a year later under the Treaty of Guadalupe Hidalgo in 1848.) In 1896, after much wrangling with the US federal government, Utah was granted statehood and Salt Lake City became the capital. In the intervening years, thousands of religious converts had moved to the city. Additionally, large immigrant groups, particularly from Greece and Japan, arrived to work on the First Transcontinental Railroad to the north and in multiple mining industries in Utah.[20]

Before I moved to Salt Lake in 1993, I had the same impression that many people have of the city: it's where "the Mormons" live. While LDS church headquarters are located in downtown Salt

Lake, Mormons do not in fact make up the majority of city residents.[21] Furthermore, although there is religious tension between LDS members and nonmembers, it is reserved in public forums, remaining voiced mostly within like-minded groups of friends or family. Typically, people outwardly claim not to care about religious differences, though discourse among strangers often includes cues regarding "membership" status. It matters, in many ways, what side of the "religious divide" (as it is termed in SLC) one falls on. Several institutions and organizations have attempted to address tensions through community-wide programs, including one in 2004–2005 by the mayor's office called "Bridging the Religious Divide," which consisted of multiple community focus groups and conversations.

Even though this focus on religious identity exists, Salt Lake City is also a complex urban area similar to other midsize western cities such as Denver, Portland, Albuquerque, and Tucson. Though more White than some of these cities, the ethnic diversity of Salt Lake has been rapidly increasing over the last twenty years due to immigration and refugee resettlements from across the world. As are most urban centers, Salt Lake County (in which Salt Lake City is located) is divided into multiple neighborhoods that span from commanding affluence to depressing poverty. Mansions in Federal Heights dot the tree-lined streets winding into the northeastern foothills that wrap around the 1,500-acre University of Utah campus (including their Health Sciences and Research complexes), while tract homes, trailer parks, apartment blocks, and strip malls surround the main Salt Lake Community College campus in the west central area known as Taylorsville/Kearns. The north–south running interstate highway and railroad tracks bisect the city geographically, economically, and culturally. To the east is more money, more White people, and more open space. To the west, a dense mix of Latino/Hispanic, Pacific Islander, African, Asian, Eastern European, White, and Middle Eastern communities live much closer together. As the valley expands southward on the east and west sides, White, middle- and upper-middle-class suburbs sprawl up to meet mountain boundaries.

These ranges affect educational opportunities in the city as well. As in other states, the Utah public education system is continually challenged to meet the needs of ever-increasing numbers of students within diminishing budgets. While Utah ranks tenth in the nation for the percentage of overall state budget spent on public education—33.6 percent in 2010 (Davidson and Farmer), its education budget—generated primarily from property taxes—cannot keep up with the large proportion of children in the state, which leaves Utah ranking very low, often dead last, on the amount spent per student (Farmer and Davidson). Still, high school graduation rates are on par with national rates and average about 87 percent overall. Approximately 27 percent of residents have college degrees, roughly equivalent to other southwestern urban areas.

Even so, these statistics mask a significant discrepancy in educational achievement among different communities in Salt Lake County. Graduation and dropout rates vary widely based on geography and ethnicity. The Salt Lake School District, which supports Salt Lake City, graduated 69 percent of all students in 2009, while the four suburban districts in the county all graduated higher than 84 percent (with one district graduating 91 percent). Dropout rates in the city double or quadruple those of the suburban districts at 8 percent (equaling the 2008 national average). Binding geography to poverty and ethnicity widens the gap even further. In the Salt Lake School District, roughly 50 percent of students come from economically disadvantaged backgrounds, and the district has the highest percentage of students of color in the county. African American, American Indian/Alaska Native, and Hispanic/Latino students graduate fewer than 60 percent of their cohort groups, and only 56 percent of economically disadvantaged students complete their diplomas. In contrast, White students in a suburban district graduated 93 percent of their cohort with only a 2 percent dropout rate (Park). In addition to a religious divide, there are, predictably, economic and color divides in Salt Lake.

While Utah might be considered one of the most politically conservative states in the United States, Salt Lake is a politically liberal city that has elected Democratic party mayoral candidates consistently since the 1970s. In fact, one of the most public critics of the George W. Bush administration was Salt Lake's former mayor Ross "Rocky" Anderson, who championed sustainability, equal rights for homosexuals, adequate health care coverage for all, and education. This phenomenon, of a progressive urban island in a conservative sea, is dotted across the western United States, including Bozeman, Montana, and Boise, Idaho. Perhaps remarkable to those who live outside the city, Salt Lake has an active LGBT population that sponsors an annual Pride Festival averaging more than 25,000 attendees. A local listener-supported community radio station, KRCL 90.9, airs fifty-six different diverse music programs and twenty-six public affairs programs (including Amy Goodman's *Democracy Now!*) each week. Bicycle and art collectives, farmers' markets, gallery strolls, environmental groups, and brew pubs mark Salt Lake City as a liberal western urban space.

Within that urban space, from 2001 to 2005 the Community Writing Center was located a handful of blocks west of downtown Salt Lake City, across from the city's homeless shelter (I discuss this location more in the next chapter). In 2006 the Community Writing Center became a tenant of the SLC Library Main Branch, a 200,000-square-foot graceful composition of glass and concrete, which "embodies the idea that a library is more than a repository of books and computers—it reflects and engages the city's imagination and aspirations" (SLC Public Library). Paid for by a voter-approved bond, the library is located on an entire city block, half of which was preserved as public green space anchored by an open plaza (known as Library Square) looking westward across the street to the Gothic Revival architecture of the City–County Building. Eschewing the notion of a "quiet" library space, library administrators encourage the noise that reverberates continuously throughout the four-story-high Urban Room public space and into the study carrels that sweep along three floors of windows looking north and east toward the Wasatch Mountains. At the bottom of the Urban Room, library patrons can visit a local café, a deli, an artist co-operative gallery, a garden and floral boutique, a library retail store, and a co-operative shop selling locally made clothing and goods. Just outside the library proper, in a swooping winglike structure that frames Library Square, a local National Public Radio station and a comic book shop neighbored the Community Writing Center.

As well as being a part of the community, the CWC was a part of Salt Lake Community College. SLCC was formed in 1948—a product of the GI Bill—as the Salt Lake Area Vocational School and has grown into thirteen campuses throughout the Salt Lake metropolitan area. (During the time of writing, SLCC became the largest public institution of higher education in Utah with more than 60,000 students). SLCC provides a wide range of general education and academic transfer programs while maintaining a broad Career and Technical Education and Apprenticeship program. Students can earn associate degrees or select from more than 100 certificate and licensure programs. In addition, SLCC provides services for business and industry through multiple training and continuing education programs. As a "comprehensive community college," SLCC responds to nationwide calls for streamlining the school-to-work path for students and makes significant investments in workforce development programs. The college also heralds its "most diverse student body" in the Utah System of Higher Education, with 16.9 percent of credit-bearing students coming from ethnic minority backgrounds, though one of its ongoing priorities is to recruit and retain a more diverse student body. Nine schools house the academic, apprentice, and applied technology departments and divisions; over the years, the Community Writing Center reported to a specific campus's executive dean, the associate academic vice president, and the dean of the School of Humanities and Social Sciences.

Like many other institutions of higher education, SLCC has moved toward a more corporate structure, apparently in response to challenges faced by exponential growth. When the CWC opened in 2001, two vice presidents and four deans administered all departments and disciplines at the college, supported by division chairs and department coordinators. Now the college's administration is more layered, with five vice presidents (one provost among them), multiple assistant vice presidents, deans, and associate deans. Common to institutions undergoing such growth and change, along with decreasing resources and statewide budget cuts, the community college experiences its share of disagreement and contention.

Within this environment, however, SLCC was dedicated to working with the community, including through award-winning service-learning initiatives and innovative business/industry partnerships. The SLCC Community Writing Center was one outcome of this commitment, coming to fruition as the college asserted its identity as "the community's college."

I understand that some (perhaps many) may find it surprising (or unbelievable) that a community college would fund a community writing center, especially through hard budget times. Some I've talked to, especially those in colleges and universities, have insisted that Salt Lake Community College is somehow "different" from their institutions, perhaps as a way to comprehend the CWC's development and sustainability. I don't believe that is the case, however. SLCC's budgeting mechanisms and decision-making systems are similar to those of most other large two-year higher education institutions, as well as those of many universities for that matter. Its budget is not more flexible than other two-year colleges funded by the state, tuition, grants, and donations. In fact, the Utah legislature's allocation process results in chronic underfunding since it is based on previous year student totals, not current levels of enrollment. The Community Writing Center was born, and grew, within a public institution quite similar to those at which most activist scholars/faculty try to do their work. It evolved in an urban environment that shared much with other urban spaces, yet also developed distinctly within the particulars of Salt Lake City. In the end, there was nothing magical or terribly unusual about the CWC's particular environments that made it possible for the center to emerge or grow.

Even so, the SLCC Community Writing Center was unusual among similar community-based writing projects. It was sponsored by a community college, not a university; it was staffed by undergraduate students, not graduate students; it sustained a broad range of writing and educational programs with many partners over many years; and it became a highly respected and widely recognized institution "writing *with*" the Salt Lake community. Actually, "writing *with*" the community doesn't quite sound right. I find it more accurate to say that the "*community wrote*" with the CWC, and in doing so created a hybrid space, one that sustainably merged community and academic discourses and generated new understandings of rhetoric, expertise, change, and institution. The specific convergence of histories, theories, intentions, and people behind the CWC allowed it to develop in ways it might not have been able to do in a different time or place. In the next chapter, I attempt to trace these convergences and inquire into the "how" and "why" of the CWC's ways of being in relation to others and to writing.

2

Evolving a Discursive Ecology: A Rhetoric of Respect

"But what if I don't know how to write?"
"You know more than you realize."
"But what if I do it wrong?"
"'Wrong' is relative. We'll figure it out."
"But when I write, it doesn't come out like I want it to."
"That's normal."
"But what if I mess up?"
"You will. And it will be okay."
"But my teachers told me I was a bad writer."
"They were wrong."

IN THE AREA OF ECOCOMPOSITION THAT MOST interests me, scholars examine writers and texts functioning within discursive ecologies, which Dobrin and Weisser articulate as follows: "Writers' structures and functions are determined, not by genetics per se, but by knowledge and ideology which functions much as DNA does; ideology and culture map (if not control) our thinking and actions much like genetic code" (73). In the production and consumption of writing, the interrelatedness of discursive organisms and their environments develops a discursive ecology—which then continues to inform the discourses that circulate within it (65–69).

At the SLCC Community Writing Center, a particular discursive ecology evolved that I have often thought of as a *rhetoric of respect*. Respect differs from sometimes patronizing responses to difference or conflict (e.g., "tolerance" or "acceptance") that mask simmering disdain. Respect implies a different type of relationship, one that is grounded in perception of worth, in esteem for another—as well as for the self. Even so, respect does not require agreement or conciliation—as "tolerance" suggests; rather, it entails recognition of multiple views, approaches, abilities, and, importantly, limitations (especially our own). In other words, respect needs flexibility and self-awareness. Engaging within a rhetoric of respect draws attention to how we use language in relation with others: how we name and classify, how we collaborate, how we problem-solve. Whereas respect itself may exist as a feeling, a rhetoric of respect requires discursive action.

At the Community Writing Center, we tried to infuse a rhetoric of respect through all our interactions; between the directors and the staff, between staff and writers, between the center and partner organizations, and among writers. Although it wasn't yet termed as such, this rhetoric is found in early CWC documents that presented programs in a "fuzzy" manner, specifically "unformed," so that multiple participants—community members and student employees—would play a meaningful role in determining what the CWC would become. In early 2000, a proposal to SLCC administration outlined the overview and purposes of such a center in this way:

Overview

The SLCC Community Writing Center (CWC) will serve as a site of learning, community-building and problem-solving. Located in the Artspace Bridge Projects, the CWC will serve two focus populations: individuals and local groups and/or community organizations.

Individuals: The CWC will serve individuals with specific writing needs on a drop-in basis. These needs might include letters to newspaper editors, résumé writing, advocacy letters, or community organizing projects.

Community Organizations: The CWC will sponsor writing projects that aim to solve problems within the urban Salt Lake City community. The goals of these projects range from expressing the ideas and perspectives of historically disenfranchised populations: homeless, elderly, ethnic minorities, writers of languages other than English, etc., to community writing dialogues among organizations representing the diverse communities in our city.

Purposes
- To provide a forum for the production and expression of the perspectives of traditionally disenfranchised community populations.
- To encourage community problem-solving by fostering understanding of inter-cultural relations and potential collaborations through writing.
- To promote a public understanding of the power of language and writing in shaping cultural identity and relationships.

The two focus populations—individuals and organizations—were anything but focused, limited only somewhat through organizations that worked with "disenfranchised" or "diverse" populations —tropes common to community partnership or development projects. Additionally, although programs with flexible boundaries evolved over time at the CWC, at its outset the "boundaries" were merely general ideas: drop-in writing, projects that solve problems, and forums for expression and public understanding.

Following this unformed approach persisted for many years and framed how those of us working at the CWC (directors and writing assistants) entered into relationships with community partners. The 2002 version of the CWC Writing Assistant Training Manual stated in the section "Representing the CWC Philosophy/Pedagogy":

> When working with an institution or on outreach, you must be sure to be collaborative and non-directive in all your work. Even though much of this work takes the form of workshops or "teaching," all planning and implementation must be collaborative and non-directive. Procedures to follow include:
>
> - Being sure you are actively thinking that the organization is the leader in the project, not the CWC. You must

believe that the organization is capable of knowing what they want and what is best for them and their clients. You must believe that they have ideas of what they want to happen.

- Being sure you go into planning meetings and discussion "blank." This means that you may have researched working with a particular population, or may have ideas, but this knowledge and these ideas stay in the background, only to be brought up as suggestions or ideas in response to questions.

- Being able to respond to the individual situation with grace and flexibility. Be able to maintain your composure when the conversation is confusing, in process, or even chaotic. Hold back your comments and suggestions until they are asked for.

The instructions point to the CWC's "ideological DNA," which was informed by—and continued to form—a rhetoric of respect. Entering into such a rhetoric required the CWC to maintain a solid faith in a potential partner's own capability and in their agency to determine what they needed or wanted. To avoid falling into the stance that the CWC, as an agent of higher education, "knew better" than a partner, we worked on entering into relationships with "blank" intentions, pushing our own ideas into the background unless circumstances might call them forth. Further, we made efforts to embrace the chaos and confusion of listening rather than take comfort in directing the conversation. Of course, we didn't always succeed, but the intention to do so remained central to the CWC's ideology.

I encountered threads of this ideology long before the development of the Community Writing Center on my own educational paths and in relationships with colleagues at SLCC and in the community. These strands of idea, theory, and people converged into a web that would frame the beginnings of the CWC's rhetoric of respect. As I move through this narrative in the pages that follow, I rely on the value that ecocomposition places on the "individual's position and experience" (Dobrin and Weisser 158), for I do not know how to tell a story of the Community Writing Center's ideological development without including some of my own within it.

SEEING IDEOLOGY

My first steps into the world of higher education took me to the local community college, where I flailed around for a couple of years trying to figure out what I wanted to do. Eventually I landed in English, though I didn't fit neatly into the department's core of literature and critical theory studies once I discovered linguistics at my hometown's university. Although a degree in linguistics wasn't available, I took as many classes as I could within English BA requirements. Decidedly interested in the sociopolitical elements of linguistics—rather than theory and scientific study—I gravitated toward understanding language as a tool of power, one through which societies enable privilege and wield discrimination.

Having been raised in a university town in a White, educated, middle-class family, my particular native tongue allowed me a relatively smooth path through the traditional education system, unlike the children in Shirley Brice Heath's *Ways with Words,* which I encountered in my undergraduate studies. Heath denaturalized language for me and revealed the dialectic, rhetorical, and educational privilege that I was granted by my home environment.[1] Lee Artz writes:

> We are born into conditions not of our own making; we benefit from the social relations into which we arrive; we are socialized into the mores, norms, and practices that cradle our existence. Available resources, including language, material culture, social interests, and their relations, are largely already formed when we enter a specific, historically contingent social order. (48)

As I moved through my studies, my awareness of this privilege and language's role in systemic discrimination was enhanced by the work of Brian Street and James Gee, who moved the notion of literacy away from a neutral skill-based activity ("autonomous" literacy) into an understanding of multiple "literacies"—in particular, Street's "ideological model of literacy" (Street 139). Gee's work regarding the inseparable relationships between language, behavior, action, value, and viewpoint showed me how language (and literacy) regulates boundaries of inclusion and exclusion, particularly through discourses, which "crucially involve a set of values and viewpoints in terms of which one must speak and act, at least while being in the discourse, otherwise one doesn't count as being in it" (538).

Recognizing language as ideological opened my eyes to the ramifications of "school literacies," and of "literacy" in general. I began to see beyond the democratic and/or empowering conceits publicly associated with school and education, and moved into awareness of discriminations built into their systems. This perception would inform the Community Writing Center's broad understanding of literacy and writing using a rhetoric of respect for individual concerns, rather than relying on institutional definitions. In collaboration with the first student writing assistants, we negotiated what kind of textual production would take place in the CWC's environment—in other words, "what writing was." Though the CWC was a part of the community college, which maintained certain definitions of what counted as writing, it was also part of the community. We decided that writing would include any kind of written text, in any form, at any stage of process, for whatever purpose or audience. (The single exception to this was found in the CWC policy about hate speech, which read in part, "In accordance with the values of Salt Lake Community College, the CWC will not provide assistance on writing projects that appear to incite abusive or violent responses from their audiences.") Further, the writing that we encountered would be valuable, regardless of whether it met social standards of valued text. We hoped to sow the seeds of a changed definition of literacy in negotiation with writers: it was up to writers to decide what writing and literacy were to them, not for us to tell, suggest, or imply what was important.

For example, a few years after the CWC opened, a gentleman from Cambodia came to the center each Monday afternoon for several months. He always entered quietly, sat at the table near the window, and wrote in his journal for twenty minutes. He then asked a writing assistant to read the few sentences he had written. Together they talked for a few minutes about the content of what he had written that day, not the grammar, even though his writing was transitioning from his home language into English. He wanted to talk about what he wrote, not how he had written it. This approach also grounded the DiverseCity Writing Series, which valued all writing (and attempts at writing). I believe this respect for all writing contributed to the revision of CWC writers' assumptions about who could be called "a writer" and, by extension, whose literacies were valuable. In DWS publications (and public reading events), eloquent stories written by individuals with advanced degrees and years of writing experience were presented alongside a few sentences that adult emerging readers had managed to produce. These respect-based acts perhaps contributed to the following responses to a 2009 DWS participant survey to the question, "What have you learned from the DiverseCity Writing Series?":

- A new respect for people I may not believe had abilities to understand, produce, and appreciate literature, poetry, etc.
- That writing is as open as anyone's mind.
- No matter who you are you can write.
- That a good, open writing program empowers people to tell magnificent stories.

MIGRATING AND RESISTANCE

After finishing my bachelor's degree, I left my southwestern hometown and moved to Los Angeles for a graduate program and teaching assistantship in linguistics at the University of Southern California (USC), where I quickly transferred into the English department's Rhetoric, Linguistics, and Literature program after confirming that, indeed, I was not a theoretical linguist. Here, my awareness of the power of language and literacy would become politicized. Early on, in a composition studies course, I encountered Mike Rose's *Lives on the Boundary*, in which he peels back the veils of traditional education to expose rich intelligences that often go unrecognized by those in power (e.g., teachers, administrators, education "specialists"). At the same time I was reading Rose's compassionate stories, I encountered stern warnings from "an angry book written by an angry English teacher" (Stuckey, back cover description) in a sociolinguistics course. J. Elspeth Stuckey's *The Violence of Literacy* argues that literacy cannot be divorced from other social contexts through which people are defined, regulated, empowered, and controlled—such as class, race, gender, nationality, and education—and to presume that literacy is an essentially empowering tool often results in an "idolatry of literacy" that disregards the material conditions of people's lives.

Though diametrically different in tone, Stuckey's *The Violence of Literacy* and Rose's *Lives on the Boundary* agree on the importance of how sociopolitical and sociocultural factors interact complexly with attempts to access and use literacies. Rose continually envelops the analysis of his students' literacy challenges in thick descriptions of their home lives and their work, emotional, ethnic, and economic situations. In one instance, Rose writes,

> I began to think about how many pieces had to fall into place each day in order for [Lucia] to be a student: The baby couldn't wake up sick, no colic or rashes, the cousin or a neighbor had to be available to watch him, the three buses she took from East L.A. had to be on time—no accidents or breakdowns or strikes—for travel alone took up almost three hours of her school day. (185)

Gaining access would become a central concern for the Community Writing Center, and we strove to remove those barriers we could. Free writing coaching responded to financial barriers; situating programs across the valley (not just in the center) attended to issues of location. Offering coaching, workshops, and writing groups throughout the week and into the evenings responded to time constraints. The CWC's Children's Corner, funded by a small corporate grant, invited parents to bring their children with them to the center. New barriers continually surfaced, such as a young woman who survived a near fatal motorcycle crash from which she was left unable to use a keyboard. In response, writing assistants badgered local computer shops until one donated a voice-recognition software program for her. Another writer, living at the homeless shelter, struggled with profound alcoholism and was inebriated by noon each day. Yet he was desperate to write and to share that writing with the writing coaches at the CWC. Together, we agreed that he would work with writing coaches only before 11:00 a.m., by which time he had typically consumed enough alcohol to render his behavior unmanageable. If he stopped in early, around 9:00 a.m., the smell of alcohol was like background noise, but if he arrived around 10:30 a.m., we knew we had only a short amount of time to work. The arrangement lasted for months, until he returned to his home state back east. A rhetoric of respect allowed us to work with each writer, recognizing the value and limitations that the writer and the CWC staff brought into relationship with each other.

Rose's and Stuckey's work also drew my attention to the myth of the individual writer who composes with ease and confidence. Combined with the United States' fixation with individualism, the idea of the "lone genius" discourages many from writing, much less sharing their writing with others. The possibilities of "failure" or being seen as "not trying hard enough" make the effort not worth the risk. Both Stuckey and Rose blast institutional judgment of individual performance and effort, which places blame on students and learners, as a way to rationalize the education system's failure. Stuckey argues that "American faith in individual strength and will-power" releases those in control of the system from responsibility, and within such a mindset, people "get what they achieve" on their own (3), even if systemic patterns of failure emerge. Rose critiques the "platitudes about motivation and self-reliance and individual-ism—and myths spun from them," and laments that in the end "we find it hard to accept the fact that they are serious nonsense" (*Lives* 47). Nobody succeeds, or fails, on his or her own.

Just as my primary discourse, the one I acquired from my family, set me up for a smooth transition to educational discourses, my social networks (parents, teachers, friends, employers) provided me with support and guidance in my path through educational systems and expectations. My web of relationships made it possible for me to negotiate educational literacies. These networks are well documented in Deborah Brandt's extensive work with literacy histories, in which she notes that relationships were "one of the most striking characteristics of the interviews" in that "they were filled with references to other people: teachers, relatives, friends, religious figures, military officers, librarians"("Literacy" 49). No one can enter into educational (or secondary)[2] discourses without already existing within, or becoming part of, relationships that provide access; "opportunities to know [to be literate] depend on the relationships people maintain, the types of opportunities they have to gain access to sources of knowledges, the culture and experiences they bring to learning"(Stuckey 18).

Further, Rose and Stuckey deepened my awareness of the dual—and contradictory—roles of literacy education: empowerment and control. Those with less social capital seek out literacy and education since "to be literate is to be legitimate" (Stuckey 18). However, to be legitimate, one must change, one must adapt to Gee's *"saying (writing)-doing-being-valuing-believing combinations"* deemed appropriate for particular environments. Stuckey writes that "becoming literate signifies in large part the ability to conform, or at least, to appear conformist" (19), and both Stuckey and Rose are concerned with educational systems that fail to recognize nonmainstream capabilities and intelligences. To gain power, students with nonmainstream literacies must give them up, or at least hide them from public view.[3] Stuckey writes that

> literacy is a system of oppression that works against entire societies as well as against certain groups within given populations and against individual people. The third world is oppressed by the literacy of the first world, ghetto blacks are oppressed by the American system of literacy education, and a second-grade girl is oppressed by a teacher who fails to understand the craziness of the spelling of vocabulary words. (64)

A teacher who is unable to understand, or perhaps declines to speak about, the "craziness of the spelling of vocabulary words" manifests the control that autonomous literacy holds over students in the US education system. A curriculum that breaks language use (literacy) into an analytic set of skills is "especially troublesome for [the] children" that Rose worked with, children "who had not been prepped in their homes to look at language in this dissected, unnatural way" (110). Over time, the masses of children entering school are pulled apart into stratifications that mirror discriminatory socioeconomic divisions.

As I embraced these political arguments, I also noticed that I was not adapting to the environment of graduate school. During a "Modernism in American Literature" course one winter afternoon, students were railing intelligently about the oppression of government "identity" regulations as I sat quietly, thinking of my drive home through the neighborhoods surrounding the campus—graffiti-covered walls, thick bars on windows and doors, people sleeping on sidewalks—to my rent-controlled apartment in West Hollywood, where a young woman could stroll about, even at night, without a care in the world. My identity certainly was not being oppressed, and I knew that further graduate study was not in my future. I could not stay in the world of ideas, because I could no longer switch off the material world. As Dana Cloud writes, "Criticism of prevailing ideologies and consciousness is part of intellectual work, *but critique must happen in conjunction with practical political activity if it is to be relevant at all to the democratic project*" (15; Cloud's emphasis). I didn't intend to take a vow of poverty or dedicate my life to activism, but I knew I couldn't keep listening to such critique in graduate seminars. I applied for completion of a master's degree, studied for my exit exams, and began to look at the dire job market. Luckily, before I left, James Kincaid, then-chair of the English department, told me about the USC Neighborhood Academic Initiative program.

The University of Southern California is one of the wealthiest universities in the nation, with a stunning endowment and donation record. It is also located on the corner of Vermont Avenue and Jefferson Boulevard in Los Angeles, just a handful of blocks from the intersection of Florence and Normandie, the flash point for the 1992 LA riots. The university's resources stand in contrast to the neighborhoods that surround it, though USC has leveraged its position to benefit its neighbors.[4] One of these programs is the Neighborhood Academic Initiative (NAI), a "rigorous, six-year pre-college enrichment program designed to prepare low-income students for admission to the university." Those who "complete the program and meet USC's competitive admission requirements are rewarded with a full 4.5-year financial package." The vision of the NAI, now twenty years old, is "to increase the enrollment and graduation rate of low socioeconomic, neighborhood, under-represented students to the University of Southern California" ("USC Neighborhood"). Students entering the seventh grade in nearby schools are chosen for their potential to succeed (not necessarily academic achievement) to participate in morning, afternoon, and weekend tutoring and instruction, known as the Pre-College Enrichment Academy (PCEA).

It would not be surprising if J. Elspeth Stuckey considered the NAI program a classic example of the "violence" of literacy in that it requires conforming to academic and middle-class ideologies. (For example, a student's eligibility for the program requires family members to attend regular seminars in NAI's Family Development Institute to acquire strategies to support their children's academic efforts and transformations.) While this may be true, the students and families are treated with respect, according to NAI's founder and first director, James C. Fleming; the students are "treated like star pupils. Called scholars instead of students, they are asked for their opinions on weighty issues, ranging from the Democratic National Convention to the death penalty, and they are expected to complete every bit of the mounds of homework they carry home each night" (Jones). Mike Rose, who found that low-achieving students will "float to the mark you set" (*Lives* 26), advocated for the benefits of such a challenging environment, which, in NAI's case, has led to academic success for many students: of the more than 500 who completed the program as of 2010, 95 percent were accepted at USC or other colleges and universities. The students conformed yet also reaped material benefits from doing so.

I started at the NAI the year after it launched, with just two cohort groups in the program: seventh graders and eighth graders. I taught language arts to twelve- to fourteen-year-olds in PCEA's

Saturday Academy, which took place on Saturday mornings. Even though the students had been thoroughly trained in the behaviors of middle-class classroom discourse (e.g., quietly listening, raising hands, waiting turns to talk), there was no doubt they would rather have been doing something else on their weekends. Still, they persisted, and together we shared about a dozen hours of reading and writing experiences. After I moved to Salt Lake City that fall for my faculty position, I wanted to remain part of the NAI and jumped at an invitation to return to Los Angeles the following summer for their participation in a county-sponsored education/work training program. The six-week program was intended to link "work and learning [to reinforce] basic skills education" for students in junior high and high school.[5] In NAI's project, twenty-five student scholars were "hired" to create a "Neighborhood Academic Initiative Welcome Manual" for incoming students. My job as work site supervisor was to facilitate the process, while the scholars were to write the manual. At 9:00 a.m., on a Monday morning in late June 1994, I met students I hadn't seen for a year—and who had just finished ninth grade—and we got to work.

Our first task was to understand the assignment and to write a mission statement. The scholars broke into groups, which I and a USC undergraduate student who was assisting in the project floated among. The room filled with raucous discussion, laughter, and "nightmares" of the students' own NAI experiences, mixed with their expressions of hope to make the transition easier for new students. They knew that NAI scholars had to follow certain rules, but they wanted to introduce those rules to new scholars in their own way. I encouraged this goal, wanting to recognize that they brought knowledge to this project that no one else had—not me, not the NAI staff, not their parents—and they knew how to talk to new students so they would listen. As Charles Bazerman writes about teaching working-class students in New York, "As savvy human beings they brought plenty to the classroom, but not the same things I did. So my teaching started in two places, looking at the students, what they knew and could do. Then looking at what I knew and could do. The pedagogy was to try to bring the two together" (42). This was how I wanted to spend our time together.

In the mission statement, "The Key to Success," the scholars wrote:

We, the first class of the USC PCEA, are giving what we have learned so your journey through the next six rigorous years in the Academy can be an easier and smoother ride. By writing this manual we hope to give you, incoming scholars, the knowledge you will need to get through the program. We hope that this manual teaches you how to respect each other and work as a team. As scholars in the USC academy, we have to perform at our highest level and take all of our tasks seriously. From previous experiences and examples, we are able to tell you that if you are not ready to make the commitment, then you are not ready to become a SCHOLAR.

After that, we organized. We had six weeks to determine the sections of the manual, write the content, take pictures, design and lay out the publication, and get it printed. Everyone shouted out their ideas, argued about priorities, and voted to make decisions. Together we sketched out a weekly plan with objectives and deadlines. Each scholar became a member of two different working teams: a writing team and a production team. Each writing team took on a different section of the manual—Code of Ethics, Staff, Privileges, Requirements and Expectations, Changes and Problems, Q&A—and was responsible for research, drafting, getting feedback from the other writing teams, and final revisions. Production teams broke up into Photography, Typing, Layout and Design, Final Edit, and Sales. An oversight by the NAI staff meant we had no publication budget, so the Sales Team took on the task of making proposals to program administrators for part of the costs and soliciting donations and advertising for the rest. Each work team drew up timelines and tasks, assigned responsibilities, and organized budgets for operation.

Even though we experienced both the predictable and the unpredictable problems that go along with any community writing project, especially one that employed young teenagers, overall we seemed to be engaged in a genuine collaboration. The scholars became annoyed with one another and with me, so we worked through problems in each morning's staff meeting. We got behind schedule—partially due to lack of access to enough computers for production—and by about week four, it was clear that we might not meet the final deadline. The program assured us that they would see the project through to publication if we didn't finish on time.

During the six weeks, there were only a few hints that the discursive regulation the NAI administration exerted to prepare students academically was still in force in this extracurricular program. While stopping by the workroom one day, an NAI staff member asked me to come to the office after our work ended at 3:00 p.m. It had been a good day, and I expected to be commended for the high level of engagement the scholars were demonstrating. Instead, I was given a gentle yet definite reprimand in which I was reminded of NAI program rules of behavior that were my job to enforce. Specifically, the students were not to call me by my first name and were not allowed to speak Spanish in front of me or any non-Spanish-speaking person. These were rules I had followed in the Saturday Academy, but for this six-week program I had encouraged both of these behaviors because I had been instructed to create a "work environment" rather than a school space. I had hoped that using my first name would dilute the authoritarian element in my role of boss–teacher and encourage student ownership of the project. Also, I had suggested to some of the Spanish-speaking scholars who were struggling with brainstorming in English to do it in Spanish first and then rework their ideas into English. I wanted to draw on abilities that might remain hidden in an English-only environment. My explanations did not sway the NAI staff.

The next day I reluctantly told the scholars that they had to call me "Ms. Rousculp" and always to speak in English. Out of respect for our team, I told them this wasn't my decision but that we had to make the change. Although this risked pitting the scholars against the NAI administrators, I quickly discovered the students were already miles beyond me in negotiating their relationship with the NAI program. They spoke candidly of what they were trading off (e.g., friends, family, culture, a stable sense of who they were) to gain access to material benefits. Adapting to educated, middle-class ideologies was a constant in their lives, and they made daily choices to stay in the NAI program. Enforcement of these discursive rules was nothing new to them.

At the end of the six weeks, the manual wasn't complete. Although all the writing was finished, edited, and typed, all the photographs selected and the layout designed, computer problems had prevented us from completing the entire manual. About six pages were finished and provided a template for the remaining pages. Since we didn't have the publication to distribute at the finale party, I created certificates for each of the students citing specific accomplishments such as "Most Improved Writer," "Best Organizer," "Best Leadership," "Best Problem Solver." As I drove with Keesha and Julia to the predawn produce market, where Julia's father gave us boxes and boxes of food for the celebration, I felt good. The scholars had written a useful manual that spoke in a mixture of home literacies and NAI literacies. Before I returned to Salt Lake, I submitted a final report that included explicit instructions regarding what needed to be finished. The NAI staff assured us it would happen.

But it didn't.

In the fall, I received a letter from a scholar who had emerged as a leader in the project. She wrote that the NAI staff decided not to publish the work the students had done, deeming it inappropriate for incoming scholars. It seemed they thought the manual would jeopardize the necessary enculturation of the new scholars. This program, which in other respects highly valued the capabilities and perspectives of the students, appeared to be unable to validate the students' literacies in a public document—particularly when it included thoughtful critique intended to empower newly entering scholars.[6] I called the administrator who hired me for the work-training program and argued that this decision contradicted the administration's voiced respect for the scholars. I was told that the kids had learned something while earning money; the NAI administration was satisfied with how the project had gone.

This writing project ran up against its "range of tolerance," the "boundaries of a habitat in which a species can live and survive"

(Dobrin and Weisser 75). While program administrators could entertain the idea of students writing a welcome manual for incoming scholars, they couldn't endorse its actual implementation. Anis Bawarshi also uses an ecological metaphor in his discussion of genres, which "are more like rhetorical ecosystems in which communicants reproduce the very conditions that in turn call for certain typified responses" (73). Thoughtful critique of the program, meant to empower incoming students, fell outside of the typified responses the NAI anticipated for a welcome manual. I understood the NAI's perspective, given that the welcome manual was intended to introduce the value of an unfamiliar set of discourses for incoming scholars. Still, though it was not my voice that had been silenced, it felt like I had been.

A few years later, teaching composition and linguistics at SLCC, I found myself coleading a drive to affiliate our inhouse Faculty Association with the American Federation of Teachers union, during which time Ira Shor was invited to campus to discuss his scholarship and critical activism. Through Shor, I discovered Paulo Freire. Somehow, perhaps because I switched from linguistics to rhetoric, I had gotten through a master's degree in rhetoric and composition without encountering Freire's work. Through Freire, and Shor's interpretation of his work for composition in American higher education, I found a way to enact my political concerns about literacy and education.

As I studied Freire's deep belief that "every human being . . . is capable of looking critically at the world in a dialogical encounter with others" (Schaull 32), I rediscovered the inspiration I had experienced during my undergraduate years. Moreover, Freire's work extended my understanding of how educational systems serve to maintain power inequities in a society. In response, I applied Freire's problem-posing pedagogy—specifically, Shor's interpretation of it (e.g., *Empowering Education, When Students Have Power*)—to the particular contexts over which I had control: composition classes that I taught. Along with a handful of other teachers, I did away with textbooks and embarked on a collaboratively designed syllabus and assignments with students; together we set evaluative criteria and negotiated grades. These experiments seemed successful and feedback from students was mostly positive. Yet, perhaps most important to me, as well as to the future Community Writing Center, was immersing myself in the collective uncertainty of such an approach and how it required me to shift my attitude toward composition students.

In *Education for Critical Consciousness*, Freire writes, "Teaching the technical aspects of the [culture circle] is not difficult. The difficulty lies rather in the creating of a new attitude—that of dialogue, so absent in our upbringing and education" (52). While the mechanics of collaborative syllabus design or shared evaluation can be enacted by nearly anyone, attitude is the key component of change. If I had continued to view students as incapable, unfinished beings who needed me to deposit information into them or to make them whole, I would be replicating the system I was trying to alter, regardless of my pedagogical approach. However, working collaboratively with composition students reminded me of the Neighborhood Academic Initiative project: the capabilities scholars brought to the writing project, their sophisticated analysis of the power structures they were working within, and their subtle navigation of the system's rules. SLCC students brought similar abilities with them to our classes. As I continued a problem-posing pedagogy, I absorbed the default assumption that students were indeed intelligent, critical, and capable of engaging with writing in sophisticated ways. My job was to dialogue, to collaborate, to facilitate their work toward goals that the English department had set for them. I wasn't there to tell them what to do or how to do it; rather, I wanted to help them see the problems they faced in writing and to collectively uncover ways through those problems. Without actively trying to, I had pivoted—and lost the power-laden sense of what it meant to be a "teacher." When I occasionally tried to return to this role, lecturing to students about "what a paragraph is," or Aristotelian *topoi*, I stumbled through my notes, completely awkward in a linear relationship with students. When I met with the first group of CWC student writing assistants, the attitude I had acquired through collaborating with SLCC students laid the groundwork for the rhetoric of respect that we developed together.

MAKING A COMMUNITY WRITING CENTER

During the late 1990s, Stephen Ruffus, then-writing program co-ordinator for SLCC, had been thinking about writing, literacy, and community. He had worked with youth groups and prison inmates, and imagined a place that could explore "the ways in which writing leads to and enables action, how it shapes and constructs both identity and social structures." He had been reading Deborah Brandt's work in literacy sponsorship, specifically how literacy both empowers and limits human beings—depending on the social, economic, and political contexts (or environments) of their lives—and how relationships with "sponsors" play a regulating role in that process. Ruffus was intrigued with the institutionalization of sponsorship—and thus regulation—in traditional education systems. This, along with his interest in what the Community Literacy Center was doing in Pittsburgh, led to his desire to develop a center for the Salt Lake community. He first considered a center at SLCC and then wondered if partnering with the University of Utah might have more potential. He contacted Susan Miller, U of U professor of rhetoric and composition, who—in an intellectual convergence—had also been thinking about community and had begun working toward an ultimately approved literacy studies minor housed in the university's writing program. The two began a series of conversations about creating a public literacy center.

At the same time, Ruffus was playing tennis. He did this routinely with a group that included his long-time friend Stephen Goldsmith, the founding director of a local neighborhood-building nonprofit organization, Artspace, Inc. Artspace, founded in 1980, "creates affordable live and work space for artists, cultural organizations, non-profits and others to revitalize and promote stable, vibrant and safe communities" ("Artspace") and, at that time, had already established two vital projects in an area of Salt Lake City that seemed to have been lost to crime and drugs. The first recycled an old farmers' distribution warehouse into artist studios and living spaces; the second emerged just across the warehouse parking lot and turned an old tire and rubber production plant into affordable apartments (zoned for workspaces) with retail and nonprofit space on the first floor.

While hitting balls back and forth across the net, Ruffus told Goldsmith about his conversations with Miller. Goldsmith said, "I've got the place for you: the Bridge Projects," a new development combining low-income living/work spaces with retail/office space located adjacent to the homeless services district. The Bridge Projects was anticipated to be the generative edge of intelligent urban development in the city. Goldsmith said he would make sure there was a space for a literacy center in the building, but first he had a favor to ask: "I've been trying to get a newsletter going for this neighborhood for years and can't seem to make it happen. Is there anything the college could do to help with that?" Ruffus said he'd see what he could do.

A few days later, Ruffus showed up in my office to ask if I might be interested in taking on the newsletter project. He knew that I was implementing critical pedagogies in my classes, and he also knew what I had done in Los Angeles with the NAI students. He thought the partnership with Artspace might allow me to combine these interests. I said yes.

In the spring of 1998, the first "Artspace Writing Project" course started out with eight students. As a class, we met with Goldsmith and other Artspace staff members, toured the two Artspace buildings, and met regularly at a café in the neighborhood. Students wrote about artists living in the buildings, a children's art cooperative, and a day care for kids living in the shelter down the street. They also wrote about the neighborhood: a Mexican civic center, a health clinic for indigent patients, and an independent radio station. Some students wanted to write about unspoken histories of the area, including those of Greektown, Japan Town, and the city's former red light district, complete with underground tunnels to move public officials safely (and anonymously) from one commitment to the next.

Together over pizza one evening, the students named the newsletter "Bridges: Building a Neighborhood through Story," and over the next two and a half years, English students wrote the stories and took the photos while students in SLCC's Printing Apprenticeship program designed and produced it as their capstone project.[7] We hand-delivered the publication to each door in the Artspace buildings, to each community organization, to each shop and café in the area. In a way, it was a service-learning partnership, even though we hadn't yet heard of service-learning as a pedagogical approach. This fortunate ignorance may have created a stronger partnership with Artspace and the neighborhood than would have been the case had the course been framed as such. The students saw themselves as investigators and storytellers, not as ambassadors of service or "good works" (which sometimes leads to problematic relationships with the community, and for the students).[8] Although we couldn't really measure whether the newsletter played a role in knitting together the neighborhood, Artspace was able to use it as a persuasive artifact in its funding drives, raising more than a million dollars toward the Bridge Projects.

While the Artspace Writing Project was going on, Ruffus and Miller invited me into their conversations about creating a center in the community. Miller had taken a draft prospectus to university administrators with the goal to "establish a community center focused on multiple users of language to improve relationships within and among groups" (S. Miller 1). Imagining the center in the community—perhaps at a Baptist church where she had connections—Miller wanted to push toward a more engaged university, shifting the traditional "import/export" model of community–academy relations, in which universities export their knowledge to local communities. The prospectus grounded the center's activities in "Education, Sharing and Understanding," with a goal to create a "physical site and visible identity under which many groups will engage in activities related to the learning, improvement and sharing of written and spoken language" (4). Over time, however, Miller began to think that the community college better recognized the potential of the CWC as a community-building investment, and she withdrew the university from the project.[9] Ruffus and I wondered whether a community college could run such a project on its own; the programs we'd looked at, like the Community Literacy Center, had graduate students, research assistants, and upper-level undergraduates as resources. A community college's resources were limited to commuter first- and second-year students, many with families, full-time jobs, and complex lives.

Ruffus and I wanted to create a space that brought together a myriad of ideas, including those of Heath, Gee, Street, Brandt, Rose, Flower, Freire, and Shor, among others. Calling it the "Center for Literate Action," we imagined how it might fit into the larger Salt Lake community and education ecosystems. At that time in Salt Lake, there were two main nonprofit adult basic literacy programs, one serving native English speakers and the other adults learning English as a foreign language. In addition, multiple for-profit and government agencies offered training in English to refugees, immigrants, and international students. Several nonprofit and government agencies provided extracurricular reading and writing programs for kids and teens but not for adults, although SLCC, the University of Utah, and the city's Adult Basic Education office offered a handful of noncredit continuing education courses in writing.

Within this environment, we found a niche for our project: working with people who could read and write but who still wanted to achieve things with writing they might not feel equipped for, or were perhaps prevented from achieving due to time constraints, cost, or limited instruction. We realized we weren't looking to address immediate functional literacy needs; instead, we hoped to provide a flexible environment in which people could determine their own needs and wants for writing, a place where perhaps people could become "self-sponsored" in their literacy development. As we continued working with each other and with community members and SLCC administrators, we realized we were talking about a writing center.

That we didn't initially see this connection was not surprising; the complex, sometimes divisive, relationship between composition and writing centers has a long history, as Beth Boquet outlines in "'Our Little Secret': A History of Writing Centers, Pre- to Post-Open Admissions." She writes of the long-standing tension between these two fields, represented in *College Composition and Communication* and *College English*, "with writing center scholars continually called on to articulate . . . the relevance of writing center work to the field as a whole, as though it were not an area as self-evident, as, say, basic writing or computer technology" (476).

By the same token, there are few references to theories or pedagogies of empowerment, public writing, or community engagement in seminal writing center scholarship. While the CWC's activities moved fluidly among rhetoric, composition, community literacy, and writing center work, these disciplinary separations confronted us when we found ourselves in the larger academic ecosystem.[10] At conferences, writing center colleagues seemed not to notice the relevance of the Community Writing Center's work to their own, and composition colleagues appeared to want to classify the CWC as a different academic species. Once a colleague disagreed with my perspective on a community project with the response, "Well, I'm coming from rhetoric; you're from writing centers." But these classifications didn't seem to apply in the SLCC Community Writing Center, where rhetoric, composition, community literacy, and writing center work came together, and where practices "shapeshift[ed]" and could "not easily be pinned down" (Geller, Eodice, Condon, Carroll, and Boquet 18). The CWC crossed the tolerances of each discipline, pivoting among them, drawing resources from each, yet not completely adapting to any.

Writing center scholarship provided a shape for how we might create a space for community writers using community college resources, specifically those concepts articulated by Muriel Harris in 1988:

- One-to-one learning environments (typically known as "tutoring," "consulting," or "assistance") are offered.
- Tutors (or consultants, peers, or others in this position) are not teachers; they collaborate or coach.
- The student's individual needs are the focus of the learning exchange.
- Experimenting and practicing are encouraged in a nonevaluative setting.
- All levels of writing proficiency and writing from a variety of courses are welcome in writing centers. ("SLATE")

The CWC would be a place of collaborative experimentation, a place to take risks without evaluation, where people from all different backgrounds could come to work on any kind of writing task. Also, complementing the literacy and educational theories that informed our desire to create a center for the community, we drew on the notion of writing centers as sites of change and empowerment rather than as "fix-it" shops or expressivist salons.[11] In the words of Harry Denny, "Foundational scholarship on writing centers pursues a[n] . . . agenda of challenging hegemonic practices and championing pedagogies of empowerment" (46).[12] Though treated as academically distinct, writing center work didn't seem so distant from the rhetoric, composition, and literacy scholarship that had brought me to this point.

One way writing centers have pulled weeds from the garden of educational power is through peer-based tutoring. Kenneth Bruffee's early arguments in "Collaborative Learning and the 'Conversation of Mankind'" describe the failure that he believes led to the development of writing centers: "One symptom of the difficulty [underprepared] students had adapting to college life and work was that many refused help when it was offered . . . [by] tutoring and counseling programs staffed by graduate students and other professionals" ("Collaborative" 637). When tutoring services mimicked a teacher–student relationship, students did not respond. To address this, some colleges turned to an alternative that was "not an extension" of classroom teaching: peer tutoring (637). These peer-based relationships resonate with Freire's appeal that "education must begin with the solution of the teacher-student contradiction, by reconciling the poles of that contradiction so that both are simultaneously teachers and students" (*Pedagogy of the Oppressed* 72). Ruffus and I recognized that a peer-based model would be possible in a center sponsored by a community college: students, who were also members of the community (and thus peers of those we imagined using such a space), could reconcile the teacher–student contradiction and at the same time make it possible to imagine the project without graduate students or research assistants. The "Center for Literate Action" became the "Community Writing Center":

not a research site, not a service site, but a writing center built on a foundation of resistance to regulatory literacy education.

Ruffus and I dove into the work of creating a space specific to the environment of the city, the college, and the Artspace Bridge Projects. To do so, I spent a lot of time at Artspace. In addition to the newsletter project, I taught summer courses for kids in Artspace's Institute for Art and Imagination and developed relationships with the staff members and community residents—and by extension, the college did as well. Ellen Cushman claims that faculty members' involvement is crucial to the success of service-learning projects, and faculty must be willing to step beyond the comfort of the classroom ("Sustainable"). Although the CWC wasn't a service-learning project, Cushman's argument still holds. When I wasn't at SLCC, I was at Artspace, leaving behind the college and moving into the community, doing what Linda Flower and Shirley Brice Heath claim are central to sustainable partnerships: "[They] demand risk taking that goes beyond stepping off campus to deliberately stepping outside one's own discourse and conceptual frameworks" (47). I sat in discussions with other organizations considering moving into the Bridge Projects development and was frequently brushed aside by organizational directors and presidents more adept than I was at negotiating how to create a space shared by a writing center, a drug-recovery center, a community mediation center, a local radio station, an antiracism nonprofit, an art gallery, a grocery store and café, all underneath three floors of low-income housing, across the street from the homeless shelter. To many of them, I was just a young teacher out of her league in community development work (both of which were true). Sometimes it was brutal to realize how little authority I held outside of the classroom, and how very uncomfortable that made me.

At the same time that we were entering the community, we had to persuade the regulators of our home environment as well: the SLCC administration. Fortunately, Ruffus and I found advocates in Dean of Humanities and Sciences David Richardson and Dean of Continuing Education Geoffrey Brugger, whose positions in those days held significant institutional power at the college. I also worked closely with the SLCC Development Office to adapt to proposal writing genres that administrators and funders would respond to favorably. (The college's grant writers teased me mercilessly about my effusive and overly conceptual academic prose.) Additionally, the Artspace Writing Project and the DiverseCity Writing Series were attracting attention. Slowly, all of these relationships began to vibrate the college's institutional web. In 1999, Stephen Goldsmith started his own efforts to secure buy-in from the SLCC president and vice presidents by inviting administrators to hold a retreat at the Artspace projects. He got them off the campus and into the city—into the "Westside" of Salt Lake, which got their attention: an SLCC presence on the Westside would show the college responding to inequities in higher education for communities of color and economically disadvantaged students—albeit in a very small way.

When it came time to make a decision about leasing space in the new Artspace building, SLCC's president said yes. I will never know exactly why. In an interview later that year, then-President H. Lynn Cundiff said, "For me, it was the opportunity to get outside of the box and teach in a nontraditional format. I think it is an opportunity to give back to the community in unique ways and to help a segment of our society that is often neglected, to say nothing of the opportunity for more traditional students to widen their horizons." I don't know what the behind-the-scenes discussions were, or if arm-twisting or deals were involved,[13] but on October 22, 2001, after almost four years of work with the community and with the administration, the CWC opened on the ground level of the Artspace Bridge Projects. Inside were a wall of donated books, a few tables and chairs, a couch, two loveseats and a coffee table built by prisoners enrolled in design and construction classes through the college, five computers, and floor-to-ceiling windows that looked out across the street to the homeless shelter. For the next year and a half, six student writing assistants and I started to build the CWC with the support of a steering committee comprising academics and community members. In an article for *Writing Lab Newsletter* on the one-year anniversary of the CWC's opening, I wrote:

It's 11:30 am. We unlocked the doors a half-hour ago and now a writing assistant is sitting across the room at a table with a homeless Native American man. He came in yesterday to work on a resume, and spent several hours "hunting and pecking" at one of our computer keyboards putting together a draft. Today, they are comparing what he has created to samples in some of our books, and are making decisions about revision. Two men who live upstairs just came down to check their e-mail. Our radio is filling the air with tunes and the sun is coming through the windows, warming away the autumn's morning chill. ("Into" 13)

Our windows opened to a contradictory view: men and women lining up at the shelter to secure a bed for the night could watch people driving in from the suburbs to shop at the new multimillion-dollar retail development known as the Gateway. "The complex socio-economy that the center resided in mean[t] that everyone [was] welcome [there], the homeless mix[ed] with the trendy in the Community Writing Center" (11). The SLCC Community Writing Center was finding its space in the Salt Lake community environment, where it would live for four and a half years.

In 2005, Melissa Helquist, who at the time was in charge of the CWC's off-site Writing Coaching program, and I met with Salt Lake City Library Director Nancy Tessman. Though writing coaching had been offered at the library for some time, its visibility had been limited, and we wanted to discuss options for promoting it. Before we had a chance to explain why we were there, Tessman asked how we liked our current location in the Artspace Bridge Projects and whether we might ever consider moving to the library, into one of the spaces that had just been vacated by a retail tenant on the plaza. We were beside ourselves. The coveted Library Square seemed completely out of our reach, even though we had been looking for a new space for nearly a year. Our location at Artspace had become somewhat unmanageable: Goldsmith had left the organization and with him went his vision for a collaborative neighborhood-building environment. Further, parking was practically nonexistent, and many people stayed away in the evenings, afraid to enter the homeless shelter's neighborhood after dark. Some of these concerns were valid—we'd had our share of run-ins that ranged from verbal abuse to physical threats, while drug deals routinely took place outside our windows. College administrators were becoming increasingly concerned even though we'd been trained by college security in how to deal with aggressive individuals (i.e., "mace and escape"). The benefits and opportunities the Artspace environment had provided in 2001 were no longer outweighing the costs and barriers.

Helquist and I had concerns about maintaining access for writers who were transient or homeless and who used the CWC as a place of refuge, work, and connection, though we realized that the one other spot in the city most amenable to this population was the City Library–Main Branch, which provided a safe public space with reading materials and job resources, not to mention warmth in the winters and air conditioning in the summers. Moving to the library seemed a natural fit for the CWC: public libraries have long "function[ed] as key sites and librarians as key supporters" of the goal of "improving adult literacy in America" (Horning 152). Though there was an initial outlay of funds for slight remodeling, SLCC administrators liked several aspects of the new location: the library provided security personnel, the rent was cheaper than at Artspace, and the site garnered terrific public exposure for the college. After about six months of negotiations and construction, the SLCC Community Writing Center reopened its doors on Library Square in January 2006.

EVOLVING A DISCURSIVE ECOLOGY

Even though the seeds of a rhetoric of respect were planted before the development of the Community Writing Center—drawing from political dimensions of literacy education and the organizational strategies of writing center pedagogies, along with Susan Miller's and Stephen Ruffus's distinct yet complementary interests in community engagement and literacy sponsorship—it took time for this rhetoric to develop into the center's discursive ecology. The following chapters explore specific manifestations of this process, but I'd like to finish this one with an early example of how flex-ibility and self-awareness played central roles in contributing to the CWC's rhetoric of respect.

In Chapter 1, I mentioned that the pilot partnership of the Di-verseCity Writing Series consisted of two work-study students and me partnering with a low-income women's advocacy organization (which I'll call Dignity for Women). In that project, my intention was to help empower the organization's members through collab-orative writing activities and public circulation of their voices. Not unlike many such community-based projects,[14] the partnership be-gan in conversations with the organization's director, during which I proposed, and she approved, a curriculum that included writing prompts asking the women to explore their sense of self, how that self belonged (or didn't belong) to the Dignity for Women's com-munity, and then how Dignity for Women impacted the surround-ing Salt Lake community. The workshop would culminate in a publication and public reading where participants could share their voices with people outside the Dignity for Women community. In the project agreement, I wrote,

> People who have been silenced by cultural, institutional, or historical forces need a safe, encouraging, and educational environment in which to create their stories. When people write about their lives, and are valued for doing so, confi-dence and personal insight grow. Analysis of the surrounding community can lead to increased interest in, and dedication to, participating in the community.

I now recognize this type of discourse as one that though well in-tentioned, certainly wasn't respectful of the women or their lives. Rather, it patronized and assumed they needed to grow their "confi-dence and personal insight," and that they were not already "partic-ipating in the community." At the time, my rhetorical purpose was empowerment—the kind based on Freirean principles—and the partnership was intended to create opportunities for the women to "remake their world through their words" as individuals and as a collective body of authentic voices—to name themselves and their community. It was supposed to be empowering; it was supposed to challenge repressive hierarchies of education. It was supposed to be great.

We first met on a Tuesday evening in Dignity for Women's office space. I handed out materials printed on cheery, bright-colored paper and presented the goals and assignments. I was tired after the meeting (teaching outside of a classroom was still uncomfortable) and also excited because I was sure this project would make a difference in these women's lives. That didn't happen. During the eight-week project, only two (maybe three) women consistently showed up, and one was only able to make it because I drove her home (her bus didn't break down as in *Lives on the Boundary*; it simply didn't run at night). I was frustrated; why didn't these women want to empower themselves? In the end, nearly everyone who started the workshop contributed something to the zine that we produced, but most ignored the writing prompts I had given them. They wrote what they wanted to.

As I talked to the director to collect feedback for the project's final report, she said that the women had appreciated the experience and enjoyed the public reading; even so, writing wasn't a priority for them. They had other things they needed to take care of: dying parents, husbands in jail, children at home, maintaining their housing, and staying relatively sane in a crazy world. In the report to the Utah Humanities Council, which had provided funding for the project, I wrote, "Being a teacher in a college environment, I had never realized how much of a luxury writing is. Writing takes time, and energy, to concentrate, luxuries that these women do not have." How could I have been so obtuse, so unaware of my privilege and assumptions, so blinkered by the idolatry of literacy that I had overlooked the conditions these women were managing in their lives? In the drive to "empower," I had forgotten what Stuckey, Rose, Freire, and Shor had taught me: people have full and complex lives outside of the time I spend with them. Further, I had approached this project in exactly the way Stuckey railed against: I had looked to a linguistic solution in response to material problems. In doing so, by questioning why the women didn't commit themselves to the writing "opportunities" we had "provided" to them, I had disrespected their abilities to make decisions about the best way to spend their time and energy.

This experience highlighted the importance of developing a rhetoric of respect at the Community Writing Center. Our response was to try to become more flexible in our relationships with partner organizations and individuals, and to embrace the uncertainty that inevitably accompanied this rhetoric. We recognized that while the CWC's mission was centered on writing and literacy, and while these were tools through which people could enact change in their lives, it was not appropriate for us to try to convince anyone that writing was more important than other actions or responses might be. CWC staff tried to remain fully aware of the complexities that people brought with them into relationship with the CWC—ever-unfolding webs of resources, needs, and desires. The people whom I—or Stephen Ruffus, or the community college—wanted to "empower" were not deficient beings requiring our educational benevolence; as such, it was not the Community Writing Center's role to lead people to "change"; rather, we needed to respect them for who, what, and where they were at a particular moment. This realization steadily altered the way the CWC would relate to the community—from seeing ourselves as a source of salvific change toward what Ellen Cushman calls "deroutinization" in "The Rhetorician as an Agent of Social Change":

> Daily interactions follow regular patterns of behavior, what sociologist Anthony Giddens terms "routinization." These interactions result from every individual re-enacting the social structures that underpin behaviors. . . . When the routine flow of events is impeded or upset, we have an example of deroutinization—of what can be the first steps to social change on microlevels of interaction. (12–13)

Disrupting routine flows within a rhetoric of respect would eventually become the discursive ecology of the SLCC Community Writing Center. Five years after the pilot DWS partnership, the CWC's Foundational Principles (see Appendix A) would attest to the micro- and macro-disruptions that we sought to be a part of:

> The CWC has historically challenged—and should continue to challenge—the following assumptions about writing and education:
>
> - That some types of writing are more valuable than others,
> - That publication validates a piece of writing,
> - That higher education is somehow separate from community education, and
> - That higher education can know what a community needs or wants without entering into full and mutually beneficial partnership with that community.

The Foundational Principles spoke to challenge, to disruption, not to empowerment or systemic change. The Community Writing Center did not alter the power of publication to validate a piece of writing, even though it published much writing that probably would not have been deemed valuable outside of its environment. The division between "town and gown" that exists in most, if not all, communities that house colleges or universities certainly persists, although inside the space of the Community Writing Center, academics and community members fused. For more than a decade, the SLCC Community Writing Center worked to deroutinize the flow of literacy education and academy–community partnerships, always striving to do so within a rhetoric of respect.

3

Transforming Energy in Pursuit of Uncertainty

"So, who does the writing coaching?"
"We all do."
"Who teaches the workshops?"
"We all do."
"Who does the partnerships?"
"We all do."
"Who runs the writing groups?"
"We all do."
"Aren't the people who work here students?"
"Yep."
"How are you sure they can do all of this?"
"We're not. But we do it together."

ENERGY IS EVER-PRESENT IN LIVING ENVIRONMENTS as organisms consume and expend it, transferring energy from and into other organisms. Trees take the sun's energy and carbon dioxide and convert them into chemical energy and oxygen. Small fish are eaten by bigger fish, which are eaten by even bigger fish (while the very biggest sea-dwelling mammals devour millions of tiny krill). Examining such exchanges can "map the operations of [a] system" (Dobrin and Weisser 79). Likewise, mapping the exchange of discursive energy can demonstrate how "ideology and knowledge flow through discursive systems" (80). For example, writers try to impact the discursive energies of a particular audience (e.g., to persuade, to entertain, to inform, to propose). Also, when consumed, texts impact the energies of the reader (e.g., spike an interest, generate new ideas, bore to tears). By examining these discursive exchanges, it is possible to locate how, or where, change happens.

Within a writing center, discursive exchange is always present. It is generally accepted that these exchanges contribute to changes in how students relate to writing. An additional commonplace of writing center work is that peer tutors/consultants/advisors also experience transformations via exchanges of discursive energy with student writers. In fact, the change potential for peer tutors is often seen as greater than that for student writers, since, as Wallace and Wallace claim, a writing center is a "hothouse of development for [tutors]" (49). Although a writing center's primary mission may be to support student writing, the students who work there are, more often than not, also situated as learners encouraged to develop their own intellectual, educational, and professional strengths.

Given that the staffing resources for the Community Writing Center were community college students, Clint Gardner and I were able to draw on this writing center discursive tradition to develop a training program for the writing assistants. The CWC would be a place of learning for them as well as for community members. Over the years, this commitment remained, as noted in the Foundational Principles, which stated that the CWC was a place "for student employees to learn to become teachers, mentors, developers and managers. Students should always be a part of the CWC staff and special efforts should be made to recruit student employees from SLCC" (see Appendix A).

At the Community Writing Center, writing assistants appeared to undergo individualized intellectual and professional development transformations similar to those that academic writing center peer tutors often experience. Most began their positions as undergraduate community college students and left with a sense of confidence and perseverance to achieve what they set out to do, going on to become lawyers, physician assistants, teachers, database administrators, social workers, researchers, and more.[1] Collectively, however, the definition of a student writing assistant—what a CWC writing assistant "was" or "could do"—underwent a fundamental transformation that required all of us to disrupt our respective identities in relation to one another.

In this chapter, which focuses on the internal discursive ecology of the CWC, I map the energy exchanges between the writing assistants and me. In doing so, I examine the deroutinization of our institutional identities—faculty/director(s) and student/writing assistant(s)—which moved the center away from a model of literacy development in which individuals pursued rhetorical certainty under the direction of a knowledgeable guide or teacher. Instead, we formed an understanding specific to our particular environment, which posited literacy as a collective activity of rhetorical problem solving, one that not only survived but also thrived in conditions of uncertainty. This change, which evolved recursively with our developing rhetoric of respect, made possible the center's dynamic adaptations to the continually shifting conditions of our work.

As I mentioned in the first chapter, upon opening the CWC, Ruffus, Gardner, and I envisioned writing assistants working one-on-one with community members on a variety of types of writing, a plan that tweaked only the environmental tolerances of who and what student writing assistants would work with, not what they would do. However, after Stephanie McKee announced that she would teach a journal writing workshop, she pivoted on an intersection of the web of institutional norms regarding what writing assistants could do. Her seemingly minor decision to "turn" a bit in relation to professional identity reverberated at the CWC for years. It led to Tina Groves, a sophomore at the college, creating the CWC's volunteer program, which was refined and expanded by four subsequent student writing assistants. Groves also developed a long-term writing partnership with the city's main mental health services institution. Joanna Sewall, Elizabeth Coleman, Jeremy Remy, and Rachel Meads, all full-time students, consecutively coordinated the DiverseCity Writing Series (which, as I mentioned earlier, was expanded by Sara Gunderson when she was nineteen years old and in her second year of general education at SLCC), which brought together more than a dozen writing groups and published biannual anthologies. Many years after McKee stepped off the strand that was established for her as a writing assistant, Alisabeth McQueen, a sophomore biology major at SLCC, transformed the CWC's public relations and marketing strategies so dramatically that at one point the center's website received more hits than any other at the college.

It was not uncommon for writers who came to the CWC to wonder about the staff's credentials, specifically, "What kind of education do they have?" In an interview, McQueen articulated this lingering doubt about learning from students: "[Occasionally] people [don't] want to work with me because I don't have a degree in writing. They won't necessarily say that I'm not capable, but they definitely want to know my qualifications." While my writing center history assured me that student writing assistants certainly were capable of working successfully one-on-one with writers, I did worry occasionally that the Community Writing Center was relying on student employees for all of its programs—surely at some point it would come crashing down like a house of cards. This worry most often surfaced after talking with colleagues at other academic institutions who, after expressing their confusion regarding why SLCC funded the CWC, would react with surprise—and then, concern— that undergraduates were pretty much running the show.

Yet, in spite of others' reservations, the writing assistants managed to do it anyway. The work they did belied the fact that they had less formal education than many of the writers they worked with.[2] The groups of part-time writing assistants who built the CWC developed curriculum for a wide range of people—senior citizens to grade school kids, college teachers to people living on the streets—in a variety of genres stretching across personal, civic, and practical writing, for which they consistently received positive evaluations.[3] They recruited, trained, coordinated, and supported hundreds of community volunteers. They responded to requests for, and instigated, partnerships with institutions ranging from the county jail, to the City Library, to drug detox programs, to elementary schools, to local radio stations, to rape recovery centers, to the statewide arts festival. They designed promotional materials, websites, and publications and staged public readings. Nearly 80 percent of the CWC writing assistants (twenty-seven of thirty-five) I worked with started as undergraduate students. Of the eight others, two had recently graduated with bachelor's degrees and were taking general education courses to get into graduate programs outside their majors. The other six were community members, only one of whom stayed on longer than six months. The CWC stood on the shoulders of full-time undergraduate students working part-time at the center.

LOCATION, LOCATION, LOCATION

As I discuss later, the Community Writing Center's discursive ecology, a rhetoric of respect, evolved along with the disruption and transformation of CWC writing assistant identity. However, other ecologies played roles as well, specifically its off-campus location. Michael Norton and Eli Goldblatt claim that community-based work diminishes "distinctions in status, so strictly enforced by academic rank and privilege," and thus makes space for students to become "leaders and mentors" when "the needs of marginalized people and the goal of social justice become the driving force" (47). Surely the community focus of the CWC influenced the shifting identity of its writing assistants, though, in hindsight, I believe location actually may have played a bigger role in the transformation we experienced. If we had stayed on campus (perhaps working "in" the community but based out of an on-campus office), the academic distinctions between us likely would have been troubled but not altered as they were.[4]

Situated in the intersections between higher education and the community, the CWC's environment disturbed the academic hierarchy between teacher and student and uncovered unrecognized potential that writing assistants brought to the center. While we identified the CWC as an educational space, our day-to-day relationships evolved similarly to those in a start-up nonprofit organization, informed by a shared drive to create something meaningful. Within such an environment, nonprofit discourses emerged, including "bias[es] toward informality, participation and consensus" (Allison and Kaye 1).[5] Another factor contributing to the nonprofit-like environment at the Community Writing Center was the diversity of emerging programs coupled with limited resources. This challenge generated a make-do approach that Thomas Wolf describes: "Unlike large corporations that are highly structured and in which roles are carefully defined and largely unchanging, the nonprofit organization is usually small enough and sufficiently understaffed that a single person may be called on to fill a number of roles and perform a variety of tasks" (89).

All of us found ourselves in such shape-shifting positions, particularly in the early years at the Artspace Bridge Projects. To manage this uncertainty, at the beginning of each semester writing assistants collectively determined who would be responsible for different goals and tasks. At the same time, to respect everyone's potential, the responsibilities changed frequently and crossed multiple areas of involvement. In the fall of 2003, for example, the "Who's Doing What" list looked like this:

Everyone
- Do writing sessions.
- Do cleaning chores.[6]
- Enter database stuff (when it is ready).
- Pull and put away writer files (and make new ones).
- Check and respond to CWC email and voice mail.
- Help writers in general.
- Staff events. (Others may come to mind, but this is the general stuff.)

Tina
- Volunteer program
- Grant-Writing Workshop
- Salt Lake City Arts Council Writing Project

Alice
- Work on writing assistance skills
- Publicity (including distribution list, PSAs, etc.)
- Assist Sara with DiverseCity Writing Series
- Help on SL Arts Council Writing Project

Joanna
- Grant-Writing Workshop
- Salt Lake Arts Council Writing Project
- Evolution Workshop

- Ghost Tales Workshop
- Filing cabinet/system and inventories
- Calendars
- Computer assistance
- Framing/signs/bulletin board

Kendra
- Newsletter
- Letters to solve problems
- Journaling
- Evolution
- Writing for gifts
- Managing blog
- Writing sessions—YWCA

Sara
- DWS publication
- DWS reading
- DWS training and scheduling
- Finish DWS grant
- Short Story Workshop
- Maintain mentor communication
- Network with community orgs.
- Research grants
- Development of curriculum for LAC group
- Lac group mentoring
- DWS book distribution
- Development of curriculum for GIFT Conference

Lyndsey
- Assist Tina on Volunteer program
- Co-CWC liaison for West View Project
- Flash Fiction Workshop
- Make "Getting Published" handout
- Develop writing assistant skills
- Work on filing system
- Collaborate on publicity

Maria

- Develop writing assistant skills
- Co-CWC liaison for West View Project
- Learn about community problem-solving dialogues
- Develop Def Jam Poetry Workshop
- Assist on current writing workshops

Additionally, as director, I provided the writing assistants with a list of my responsibilities and the goals I would work on for a particular semester; in meetings, I reported to them on how I was progressing, or not, toward those goals. Each person in the CWC interacted frequently with everyone else on projects and ideas in a dynamic web of collaboration. The energy exchanges were messy, confused, generative, and resistant to codification. This process continued for several years, until the pressures of professionalizing the CWC in its Library Square location—and responding to financial crisis—necessitated identifying specific writing assistant positions (e.g., Off-Site Specialist, Communications, Volunteer Coordinator). (Within a year of this change, a dis-ease with uncertainty began to emerge because positions held specific and long-term responsibilities. Territorial tensions stemming from assumed hierarchies soon followed.)

Drawing from undergraduate student populations to staff increasingly sophisticated and complex partnerships and projects resulted in a paradox common to nonprofit environments: engaging in work we were not qualified to do. According to Mike Allison and Jude Kaye, a consistent feature of nonprofit environments is the commitment to "do the work that is in front of [us] as well as [we] can" (7), accepting that sometimes making it up on the spot is the best that can be done. I had done that myself, positioning myself as a "director" without any training in personnel management or budget planning (an experience common to many faculty members who take on administrative roles, such as writing program administrator). Likewise, writing assistants became volunteer trainers and community teachers, creative designers, and efficient coordinators.

For an individual to scramble successfully into a new position is hardly groundbreaking, but to do so collectively and sustainably suggests a transformative environment. Writing assistants didn't learn to do their work by being trained in it (I certainly didn't know how to run a volunteer program); they (we) did it in collaboration with one another and by adapting as a group to the consistent unease of not knowing what to do. Becoming comfortable with such discomfort became central to the CWC's rhetoric of respect for staffers and for those we partnered with.

Like many students who take on employment at writing centers, CWC writing assistants moved from novice positions into expert-like roles with significant insecurities and doubts about their capabilities (Trimbur 21). Some felt nearly debilitating fear when facilitating their first workshops, faced with the contradiction between their student status and the "teacherly" role of leading a workshop. Shannon Bell, who "nearly threw up" before her first workshop, became a fiercely confident writing group coordinator at the men's county jail, combining compassion with a no-nonsense approach that motivated the participants to write, even though each visit filled her with trepidation. I had grown to love the feeling of being unsettled and uncomfortable through my collaborative teaching work. Happily, I witnessed a collective evolution of this ease-with-unease as veteran writing assistants expressed deep pleasure when they didn't know what to do in a given discursive situation. New writing assistants, however, were not similarly disposed. A bit of CWC lore evolved at the center holding that new writing assistants would (and perhaps should) feel very uncomfortable for at least three to six months, and would likely want to quit due to the constant frustration that often accompanies such uncertainty. Despite being assured these feelings would pass, Alisabeth McQueen wrote in a CWC newsletter, "I had spent my life following instructions and now, I was given the opportunity to take control and expand my position. This was a responsibility I had never undertaken before, and I was terrified" (1). Such moments of terror came to be seen as pivot points at the CWC—tenuously readied for and then celebrated when passed through.

This transformation of responsibilities and roles, along with collaborative ventures into untried and unknown territories, pushed CWC writing assistants to adapt their identities beyond those of providers of one-on-one writing assistance. The CWC was a living environment, pulsing and breathing with energy and new ideas, new people, and new relationships. During the second year of operation, CWC writing assistant job advertisements began to read:

> A CWC Writing Assistant is not a traditional "college job." The CWC is a collaborative learning environment in which the part-time staff has significant authority to make decisions, to develop programs and to determine the direction in which we grow. However, along with that freedom and authority, CWC staff also has significant responsibility to their jobs— sometimes beyond the norm of an hourly wage job. A CWC Writing Assistant is challenged and encouraged to excel and to push beyond self-expectations within an educational setting.

While I was at the Community Writing Center, student writing assistants transformed how the discursive energies moved within it; they excelled and pushed beyond my, and their own, expectations, and they kept the center going.

TROUBLING THE DISCURSIVE ENERGIES OF EXPERTISE

Although the Community Writing Center existed on intersecting points between academic and nonprofit worlds, its distinct physical location was outside of academic boundaries, as were the vast majority of our interactions. These allowed the CWC to develop a transformative discursive relationship with expertise different from that often experienced in higher education.

Developing and maintaining a culture of expertise has long been one of higher education's primary purposes, through certifying new generations of the educated class and by supporting the discovery of new knowledge through research. As such, expertise is a valuable commodity that regulates position and status internally. It also frames how higher education institutions (as organisms) develop relationships (or transfer energy) with their surrounding environments—in a typically "linear" fashion, in which "universities are perceived to export their knowledge to local communities" (S. Miller 2), or as a type of intellectual benevolence, providing much needed expertise and resources to a needy community (Cushman, "Rhetorician").

To explore this idea, I turn to Cheryl Geisler's incisive examination of academic expertise (its cognitive aspects and its social/regulating roles) in *Academic Literacy and the Nature of Expertise*. Geisler defines *cognitive expertise* as the ability to negotiate "ill-defined domains" by translating "everyday literal perceptions" into "abstract representations" and then applying "extended reasoning" to "specific case data" (60–63). Such ability is not limited to academics, as articulated in Mike Rose's *The Mind at Work*, which examines "the way we decide who's smart and who isn't" (xi). The laborers and service workers profiled in Rose's book enact the complex cognitive processes that Geisler describes. But socially, an academic and a laborer are not equals. Master plumbers may encounter complex problems as do mathematicians, and may even make more money, yet the professor is granted more cultural capital and tends to enjoy more autonomy in working conditions, due at least in part to the process through which higher education assigns status to "professions" via degree-granting systems. Geisler notes: "The rise of the American university, guarantor of [professional] expertise, almost exactly paralleled the rise of the professions in general" (73).

While a professional class developed, it was also necessary to establish a culture in which "nonexperts" would want to consume "professional expertise" and accept the benefits and privileges of the professional class. To do so, higher education had to be seen as something widely accessible, yet it also needed to ensure that not all aspirants completed their programs of study.[7] Geisler argues, "The need of the professions to establish their legitimacy in the face of early 19th-century American distrust of privilege led them to transform the academy into a seamless credentialing sequence with general education at its start and highly specialized professional training at its completion" (82). Seemingly, the "2 + 2" sequence in US higher education (two years of general education courses and two years of "major" courses leading to a four-year bachelor's degree) could both manage aspirations for upward mobility and maintain an adequate, yet limited, pool of new experts for the growing professions (79).[8]

To be sure, the hegemony of literacy expertise in higher education is not without its rivals. Writing centers call academic expertise into question, as do many activist scholars.[9] In 1984, John Warnock and Tilly Warnock's "Liberatory Writing Centers" called for a reconsideration of how discursive energy moves within a student-novice/teacher-expert relationship through the writing center, aiming to restore authority to student writers. Additionally, the premise of Linda Flower, Elenore Long, and Lorraine Higgins's work at the Community Literacy Center (CLC) in Pittsburgh was the need for an alternative discourse that belonged to neither the university nor the community, creating instead a new hybrid discourse that incorporated multiple sources of expertise. In an article with Brice Heath, Flower claimed that the CLC revealed "ways to challenge some traditional assumptions about where expertise 'naturally' resides in a community/university relationship" (53). Further, Ellen Cushman, in *The Struggle and the Tools*, demarcates complex rhetorical and analytical acts (what Geisler would denote as expertise) that "uneducated" individuals use to "perceive and critique hegemony from their own critical vantage points using their own vernacular" (xix).

Even so, the range of tolerance for an inclusive sense of expertise is narrow in higher education. In a recent call for proposals I was given to review, a call that attempted to "bridge the divide" between higher education and the community, university faculty were encouraged to submit proposals for projects "based on . . . faculty expertise to benefit groups and individuals throughout the community." Additionally, as Norton and Goldblatt write, "the higher education culture emphasizes discipline specific research agendas and pedagogies driven by 'experts' in academic fields. [As a result,] individual faculty often resist pursuing research and pedagogies beyond the scope of their particular disciplines, let alone collaborating with 'non-experts' in their local communities" (42). Materially, too much is at stake for faculty seeking tenure to push the boundaries of what might be considered expertise. Correspondingly, there are few mechanisms within higher education to recognize expertise that exists outside of academic certification. Mark Lyons gets at this disjointedness in an interview with Goldblatt and Manuel Portillo,

with whom he worked on the Open Doors partnership in Philadelphia:

> I would love to see the university legitimizing skill sets you
> find in a neighborhood like North Philadelphia. . . . [Manuel]
> has remarkable skills; he could teach many classes at Temple
> from what he's learned. People in this community have skills
> to teach and organize and run organizations, but they don't
> have the degrees that are required in the university. (Lyons
> and Tarrier 57–58)

Within an academic environment, a degree signifies expertise and
therefore—outside of exceptional circumstances—a person needs
a specific type of degree, in a specific type of discipline, to be considered capable of succeeding in a particular position or role. The
"food chain" metaphor that starts out this chapter may feel familiar
to those who seek to survive—and those who thrive—in academic
environments.

While academic writing centers complicate this ideology by
the mere fact that peer tutors work in a substantial percentage of
them, a consistent regard for expertise emerges in writing center
discourse. Because they exist in academic environments, student
writing centers understandably must participate in the academic
regulatory systems within them to survive. For example, even if
a tutor disagrees with a teacher's interpretation or assessment of a
student's writing, questioning faculty expertise is not a sanctioned
activity for writing center staff—not even for the director.[10] And, as
academic organisms, some writing centers construct civic/commu-
nity engagement work as "a way of extending our expertise into the
community" (Bergmann 161). More problematic, as much as writing centers argue that their discursive ecologies disrupt "teacherly"
hierarchies, Judy Gill's analysis of tutor training manuals reveals
linear and didactic training practices, full of directives and admo-
nitions of what a tutor should and shouldn't do, despite appeals
from writing centers scholars such as Muriel Harris, who argues
that training should be modeled on tutoring sessions themselves:
building rapport with new tutors, collaboratively setting training
agendas, and valuing divergent voices and opinions ("Using").

Tutor training textbooks,[11] training manuals, academic training courses—the tools that institutionally certify the ability to work in a writing center—are the discursive outcomes of writing center maturation inside of academic environments.

Early on in the development of the SLCC Community Writing Center, before we knew for certain that it would become a place, Kendra Warren, a student intern, was developing a handout that we thought we might use in the center. We talked about how writing the handout might be approached and then I turned the project over to her. When Warren returned with her draft, I made suggestions for how it might be improved and tried to do so collaboratively, mindful of my experience with the scholars in the Neighborhood Academic Initiative. She came back again with a revision. Warren's work still didn't seem right to me, so I asked her to try again. A few days later she returned with what she thought was a finished product, but I still didn't like it. The instant I spoke with some hesitation about the document, Warren interrupted, "You say that I can do this, that I can write this stuff, but you really don't think I can. You just want me to figure out what you want and then write it that way. Why don't you just tell me what you want me to do and I'll do it? Or better yet, do it yourself." She was absolutely right. I apologized and told her I would do it myself. Though I had thought I'd changed my attitude toward the teacher–student relationship, I actually hadn't; there was quite a gulf between pedagogical principle and actual practice. As Kenneth Bruffee points out,

> Most of us count "class discussion" one of the most effective ways of teaching. The truth, however, is that we tend to honor discussion more in the breach than in the observance. The person who does most of the "discussing" in most discussion classes is usually the teacher. Our discussion classes have this fateful tendency to turn into monologues because underlying our enthusiasm for discussion is a fundamental distrust of it. ("Peer" 10)

Clearly, I didn't trust Warren's interpretation of the task I had set out for her, and as a result, I sucked the discursive energy from her, draining her confidence and trust in both herself and me. Entering a new environment on the edge of academia's "web" would alter this as the writing assistants and I had to share energy within a rhetoric of respect for one another in order for the CWC to survive.

RESPECT FOR RHETORIC BEGETS RHETORIC OF RESPECT

Soon after the CWC opened, the student writing assistants began the transformation of their academically based "tutor" identifications. In turn, I had to concretely enact my imagined sense of myself as a teacher who respected students as capable rhetors. I began to recognize their abilities to negotiate complex situations, to problem-solve, even if they didn't do so exactly as I might. I began to realize that they were already rhetorical organisms, navigating texts and discourses with increasing confidence, as long as I didn't squash their energy with my directorial power. Our developing interactions and relationships transformed the CWC's discursive ecology into one that relied on collaborative rhetorical problem solving rather than accumulation of theory and praxis.

Turning back momentarily to Geisler's analysis of expertise in higher education, it is important to note the absence of rhetoric that she uncovered. Geisler argues that in a 2 + 2 sequence in higher education—and in K–12 education—literacy practices that students typically engage in "separate expertise into two distinct dimensions of knowledge[,] . . . the 'domain content' problem space and the 'rhetorical' problem space" (84). In school, for the most part students engage primarily in the "domain content" space. Along with content knowledge, however, experts also must know how to consume or produce that knowledge according to discursive and rhetorical boundaries. The relative absence of the rhetorical problem space, save basic contextual elements (e.g., date of publication, author affiliation) in student literacy tasks, creates a particular relationship between students and teachers or texts: students get knowledge from them but do not participate in knowledge production (Geisler 81).[12] The path of discursive energy in these environments is typically unidirectional: from teacher to student.

Granted, there are several pedagogical movements that attempt to open up space for students to participate in the production of knowledge and to engage rhetorically with literacy tasks: service learning, writing across the curriculum, critical pedagogies, and portfolios/e-portfolios all respond to the linearity of much educational practice. Yet the bulk of literacy practices separate out the rhetorical problem space, and as Geisler argues, "knowledge is packaged in exactly the way that it will be most likely to be ignored or misunderstood by students," who thus develop a learned incompetence over time; students learn that they "do not, and cannot, understand" (90).[13] In the absence of rhetoric, many students remain mystified about literacy practices, as described by Mike Rose:

> [Students] open their textbooks and see once again the familiar and impenetrable diagrams and terms that have stumped them for years. . . . There is . . . embarrassment and frustration and . . . some anger in being reminded once again of long-standing inadequacies. No wonder so many . . . finally attribute their difficulties to something inborn, organic: "That part of my brain just doesn't *work.*"(*Lives* 31)

Of course, this is not true, as one distinction between novice and expert writers can be found in rhetoric. Linda Flower and John R. Hayes note that experts engage with the rhetorical problem space of a writing assignment in much more complex ways than novices, suggesting that "good writers are simply solving a different [rhetorical] problem than poor writers" (30).[14] Removing rhetorical problem spaces in education contributes to the fantastical thinking of "brains not working" or ascribing "natural talent" to those who write well. One end result of this process is that writers learn to see themselves as incapable both in and out of school. Many holders of symbolic expertise (e.g., a degree or a professional position) still consider themselves (and their colleagues, or more likely, subordinates) incompetent writers, whereas the real challenge may lie with a lack of awareness of rhetorical problem spaces.

A telling example of this disconnect comes from a 2008 partnership I participated in with the Community Writing Center, when we were approached by the Indian Education Office (IEO) at the state Office of Education. They were drafting a statewide education plan for Utah Native American Indian/Alaska Native (NAI/AN) students, from preK to adult education. I met with the IEO special-ist, Mike Benally, who had recently taken the position after many years as a teacher and principal in tribal schools around the West. The IEO Advisory Committee—teachers, professors, counselors, and administrators from around the state—had been working on the document for nearly five years; however, a new mandate re-quired it to be revised to complement the state's Minority Student Achievement Plan (MSAP) before it could be approved.

In our meeting, I asked Benally how the current NAI/AN docu-ment needed to be changed. He responded that it needed to be written "in paragraphs," to "provide evidence," and to "have rea-sonable goals." While the last two concerns could be considered rhetorically, the first one surprised me—certainly the authors wrote in paragraphs? Indeed they had; only the objectives were bulleted. Benally's articulation of the document's problems was similar to the sometimes reductive descriptions of student writing from faculty: "Their grammar is awful!" or "They just can't write!" I attributed Benally's description to a limited knowledge of the rhetorical prob-lem space in writing and asked him if I could compare the NAI/AN draft with the approved Minority Student Achievement Plan to see how we might approach the task.

Although the two documents contained similar calls for im-provement in the education system, they differed significantly in their rhetorical approaches. The MSAP's thematic basis was "A Framework for Success" and called for action items such as "Us-ing Data to Inform Decisions" and "Collaborating with Parents and Families," which crossed educational levels and assigned re-sponsibilities to different units or persons, including "Local School Boards," "Teachers," and "Counselors." The NAI/AN draft was predicated upon a graphic depicting an American Indian compass pointing north, south, east and west, surrounded by a rainbow en-closing a circle and triangle to indicate tribal diversity and strength. Further, the NAI/AN draft was organized by educational level (i.e., Early Childhood, K–12, Higher Education, Adult Education). The two documents differed in their tone and apparent relationship to their intended audiences. The MSAP was upbeat throughout, with pictures of smiling children, direct action statements, and empirical research verifying an "achievement gap," though it did not include commentary regarding systemic inequities in the education system. On the other hand, the NAI/AN document was presented in a way that assumed the audiences already understood, and thus wanted to reverse, the failures of the education system for NAI/AN students; evidence of injustices were made by anecdote and example, the authors perhaps considering empirical evidence unnecessary. The NAI/AN document denoted outcomes with quantitative measures, whereas the MSAP relied on conceptual "should" statements that could not be empirically measured.

When I met with Benally, I described the rhetorical differences between the two documents and proposed that I facilitate a similar analysis with the IEO Advisory Committee, which could then decide how they wanted to revise their document. He was worried about the committee's response when they learned they needed to revise yet again and thought telling the committee "what to do" would work better. He believed that I needed to use my energy as a "writing expert" to direct the participants through their discursive production. When I explained that the principles of the Community Writing Center wouldn't allow me to do that even if I had wanted to, he agreed to let me try.

The day of the workshop I felt the way a new CWC writing assistant felt—a bit terrified. I was younger and less formally educated than many of the participants, had less experience (most had been in education for more than twenty years), and certainly was not trained in statewide education policy. With twenty-five people staring at me, I introduced myself and the CWC, explained what I was there to do, and passed out the agenda. When I asked participants if they would mind introducing themselves, they remained silent as they looked at Benally and then back at me. In the most respectful tone she could muster at that moment, a woman in the front row asked, "Just what do you expect us to do?"

I tried to explain that the state office wanted them to revise their document to complement the MSAP document so that it could pass through the approval process and into implementation. Irritation rose from the tables: "We just did this two years ago!"; "They won't approve it anyway"; "What a waste of time." Two years prior, they had worked with a consultant to produce the current document, which went nowhere within the system. They argued that their document was fine, and resentment started to gain traction. I asked if I could interrupt. When they paused, I said, "Look, obviously, I don't understand what you are experiencing as a group; it would be disrespectful of me to presume that I did. . . ." One woman spoke up and said, "We've worked on this for so long." I said, "I know, that's what I'm trying to say. Though I can't know what you are experiencing exactly, I do know what it is like to try to get a document through a bureaucratic system that takes the humanity out of humane projects." I told them about trying to get the CWC started, about dozens of documents that were rejected again and again for reasons I didn't quite understand until I became more aware of discourse constraints outside my familiar contexts. I explained that the issue was rhetorical and not about content—they knew what they wanted to say, but they were saying it differently than those with authority wanted them to. I said that I was there to help them uncover these differences so they could decide what they wanted to do.

Though people were frustrated, they were willing to stay. I showed them my initial observations of the rhetorical differences between the MSAP and their own document. Then we began to share energy: we collaborated on rhetorical interpretations of the documents using language they were familiar with, and we recognized the particular discursive goals they had for their document. For example, it quantified outcomes yet did not assign responsibility to any educational unit or position, which countered the MSAP document's approach. They explained that they wanted outcomes they could measure because they were tired of broken promises and were also uncomfortable assigning responsibility since often the positions (i.e., teachers and counselors) didn't have the power to enact programs. They also resisted the MSAP's insistence on empirical evidence because to them the inequities should have been glaringly obvious to anyone who was willing to see them.

About a month later, we met again in another daylong rhetorical investigation. Committee members had created rhetorical frameworks for each section that did not parallel but did reflect those in the MSAP. At the same time, however, they had held onto their discursive integrity, including maintaining the compass-and-rainbow graphic and placing a statement on Native American/American Indian sovereignty at the front of the document, making sure that it informed everything contained therein. About eight months later, Mike Benally came into the CWC smiling broadly. In his hands he was holding the approved final document.

In academic environments, the rhetorical problem space is often absent until advanced levels of instruction. However, mapping discursive exchange at the Community Writing Center shows the intentional incorporation of rhetoric throughout a writing assistant's time there. In fact, rhetoric was *the* starting point for training new writing assistants. Instead of presenting it as content or concepts (e.g., "ethos, "pathos," "logos," "audience," "writer," "purpose"), new writing assistants were asked to recognize the rhetorical strategies they already enacted. A typical first twenty minutes of training new writing assistants included an introduction to the center, its mission statement, and the programs, and concluded with a question: "You've been listening, nodding, taking notes, asking occasional questions. How did you learn how to do this?" Predictably, the most common responses were confused looks and uncomfortable smiles. But I would press them: "Seriously, how do you know that you're not supposed to make demands of me right now? That you're supposed to sit quietly and nod approvingly?" At that point, perhaps questioning the wisdom of their decision to work at the CWC, they would stammer something like, "We don't know. We just do." It was then that I introduced rhetoric and rhetorical problem solving and drew connections from their navigation of that immediate discursive space to their innate ability to do so in other contexts. The CWC Training Manual also introduced rhetoric in a similarly accessible manner:

> Everybody analyzes and responds to rhetorical situations, whether they are aware of it or not. For example, when you

are talking with someone, you follow certain conventions, rules, or assumptions that will make the conversation generally go smoothly (unless you are trying to start an argument or there is confusion). A very simple example of this is when you are eating out. Usually a server will approach your table, hand you menus, and ask if you would like anything to drink. You often respond with "Thanks" for the menus, and order water, soda, or whatever else you want. The server then goes away, gets your drinks, and comes back for your order.

You and the server are analyzing the rhetorical situation while it is occurring and are responding in ways that seem appropriate to the situation in order to reach your individual goals or purposes. The server wants to provide you with a pleasant dining experience, wants to appear friendly, and, ultimately, probably wants a good tip. You want to have a nice meal, a moment to choose your food, and pleasant service. You are both operating within the accepted conventions of this particular rhetorical situation.

Now, if a server approached your table and said, "Whaddya want?" without giving you a menu, they are probably breaking the conventions of the rhetorical situation, and might not get a good tip. In fact, you might leave the restaurant for another. However, the key word here is "might" because it all depends on the context of the rhetorical situation.

"Whaddya want?" could possibly be an appropriate message from a server. If, for example, you are a regular at a restaurant, and the menu items are posted on a chalkboard instead of on individual menus. You approach a bar to order your meals and are familiar with the server, who smiles upon seeing you. In this case, the question may not sound rude or impatient, but is the convention that is followed in this specific rhetorical situation. (Rousculp, Gardner, Lund, Remy, and Sewall 11)

Some may cry foul to see rhetoric defined so reductively. Nonetheless, CWC writing assistants were not being trained to be experts in rhetorical theory. Nor was it my goal that they be placed on a path to enter a particular professional community, an assumption sometimes made of student writing center workers, whose training "invoke[s] a kind of knowledge—the theory and practice of teaching writing—that pulls tutors towards the professional community that generates and authorizes such knowledge" (Trimbur 27). Rather, CWC writing assistant training was intended to raise awareness of their ability to negotiate rhetorical problem spaces, an ability that would equip them to work with community members on their writing. It was to provide them with the tool of awareness, with which they could navigate the unease of not knowing what to do.

Now, I don't want to suggest that a brief glimpse of everyday rhetorical navigation was enough to immediately transform writing assistants into confident collaborators with community writers or self-assured workshop facilitators. As noted earlier, it took time for writing assistants to develop this ease. Yet a respect for rhetoric, for the rhetorical abilities they brought with them to the CWC, was the foundation for the collaborative exchange of discursive energies among all of the staff. Echoing an apprentice relationship, energy passed along new and experienced CWC writing assistants and me in continual meta-discussions of particular discursive moments: How did one negotiate the rhetoric of a written text within the rhetorical problem space that exists between the writing assistant and the writer? What if a workshop facilitator didn't know the answer to a question, particularly if that facilitator was just eighteen years old and the participants were in their forties? How did one explain the CWC's principles to an organization that seemed to want to be told what to do? The conversations rarely concluded with easy answers. The way that I, as the director, might respond to an organization could inform, but not provide a conclusive response to, how a new writing assistant might navigate that problem. Collectively, we settled into the continual movement that comes with uncertainty, knowing that the anchor of rhetorical examination would keep us moored to the CWC's principles.

Within a combined set of relationships, it appeared that the environment and location of the CWC, along with a respect for rhetoric, shifted the way the teacher-director and student writing assistants exchanged energy. Rather than staff members consuming or being consumed, a collaborative contribution to sharing (in order to generate new) energy became the norm, disrupting academic notions of students as nonexperts. The CWC's discursive ecology evolved from a conscious grasp of everyone's ability to negotiate rhetorical problem spaces, regardless of institutional symbols of ability or expertise. Another way of looking at this is what James Gee refers to as "mushfake" discourse,[15] wherein people can "make do" with partial acquisition of a new discourse coupled with meta-knowledge in order to navigate within it. I liken Gee's "meta-knowledge" to the awareness of rhetorical problem spaces, which makes it possible to collaborate with others in unfamiliar literacy situations. To navigate unfamiliar literacy tasks, two resources seem to be necessary: (1) meta-knowledge of the existence of a rhetorical problem space and (2) access to a partial understanding of the discourse within which someone is trying to act, through collaboration with others.

When Sara Gunderson wanted to expand the DiverseCity Writing Series into a multigroup, year-round program, she had no idea where to start, and frankly, neither did I. Together we broke down the discursive problem into parts: Who would be involved and why? What were the purposes of the DWS and how would we communicate them to different audiences (writers, funders, volunteers)? What ways did other organizations approach community writing projects and how did those methods complement or conflict with CWC principles? Even though this may seem like basic program planning, it was also a transformation of how Gunderson and I exchanged discursive energy. Neither of us had the answers, so we turned to collaborative rhetorical problem solving that respected what we each brought to the program's development—and over time, what volunteers and writers would bring to it. For years the DWS continually shifted and flexed in response to the new ideas and energies that scores of people brought to it, changing group dynamics, publication cycles, CWC oversight, and group identities.

Throughout this process of disrupting identities, student writing assistants deroutinized their attitudes toward expertise: they could do meaningful literacy work even if they had not been sanctioned by a degree to do it. This was not a simple attitude to take nor an easy transformation to make. To accomplish this shift, writing assistants had to enter into the vulnerable space of Ellsworth's pivot point, to be "in the process of losing something of who [they] thought [they were]" (*Places* 16). They could no longer remain in a safe student environment where they were not expected to be able to make their own decisions when the "right" response was uncertain. I believe the terror that Alisabeth McQueen identified—that many writing assistants experienced—was the exposed vulnerability of this transformation.

As the writing assistants took ownership of their abilities, I too experienced transformational losses. One of these was when writing assistants insisted that the volunteer training manual sounded "too academic." Perhaps because part of my identity (my certainty of my self) was an academic one, I wanted to hold onto what was left of that document's academic discourse (it had been whittled away slowly with each revision over the years). So I stopped their energetic insistence to revise it using my position as director. But they persisted for weeks. I thought they were wrong. They continued to argue with me. Not until I recognized my personal motivation for the discourse's maintenance could I recognize that the writing assistants (not I) had developed and maintained the volunteer program since its inception. My arguments stemmed from my own need for others to value academic knowledge and its dissemination. They were responding to the actual practice of training the volunteers in a community environment. In other words, the writing assistants were dealing with a different rhetorical problem from the one I was facing. Finally I made the decision to trust them to make the right rhetorical choices for the volunteer program. That decision was a significant pivot point for me because it placed me in a vulnerable space. By acknowledging that student writing assistants were the ones who made the volunteer training decisions, my own dispensability to the Community Writing Center project was revealed.[16]

A word on trust: a particular form of energy exchange among organisms in a given environment and, I believe, central to the sustainability of the CWC's rhetoric of respect. Tellingly, trust is integral to Freire's "attitude" shift imperative to the implementation of critical pedagogies. Freire writes that people in power who argue against oppression often do not actually trust the capabilities of the oppressed: "They talk about the people, but do not trust them, and trusting the people is the indispensible precondition for revolutionary change" (*Pedagogy of Hope* 60). Certainly, the CWC student writing assistants were not fomenting revolution; they were part of a micro-change—undergraduate students leading the development of a web-shaking community writing center—a process that necessitated my trust in them and their collective rhetorical abilities. They would not do it alone, but in collaboration with one another.

MIGRATING INTO COLLABORATION

In natural environments, organisms often migrate in order to thrive. They move into new spaces more suitable to their survival and, in doing so, influence the exchanges of energy within them. They cause change and are changed by their travels. Aligned with the notion of migration, Julie Drew explores the metaphor of "student-as-traveler" to argue against the construct of students as "novice, young, and, as yet, un(in)formed" (60). Recognizing that "the pedagogical is not located exclusively within the classroom, rather the classroom is one location in which pedagogical moments occur" (60), Drew argues that "students-as-travelers . . . are already engaged in various forms of critical thinking" (64), a position that echoes Freire's, Shor's, and Rose's recognition of the entire lives of learners, not just that portion that teachers may come into contact with. The writing assistants and I were travelers as well: we migrated to the CWC from different places and entered into temporary relationships with one another in a strange environment, one not fully community based nor fully academic—an instability that kept us from feeling settled and comfortable, from being certain, and forced us to be *with* one another in our work, to learn from one another, to collaborate.

In other venues, I have described the Community Writing Center as having been a fiercely collaborative space, and in this book, I have referred to collaboration often. I do not use the term lightly, simply to indicate that people worked together a lot or that everyone got to have a say in decisions. I mean it in a deeper sense, in the energetic wholeness of the relationships that made up the CWC. As those relationships pivoted and transformed, so did the center. This continual change sometimes led to chaos (as when five out of the six writing assistants graduated and moved on in the space of two months), yet it also brought ongoing creativity and new growth, flexibility, and possibilities (as when five new writing assistants started work at the same time).

A long time ago, to counter those who would question the capabilities of students to tutor writing, Bruffee wrote, "People have always learned from their peers and doggedly persist in doing so whether we professional teachers and educators take a hand in it or not" ("Collaborative" 647). *Students* learn (we hope) while they are in classroom environments, but *people* learn everywhere through interactions with parents, siblings, friends, employers, colleagues, texts, and strangers. Brandt's research documents the complex exchanges leading to literacy development that only sometimes include classroom environments ("Sponsors"). We learn through relationship with others, and over the courses of our lives, we may learn more outside of educational systems than in them. I was trained to be a teacher of composition; at the CWC, I found myself a manager of constantly shifting groups of strong-willed people. I was not prepared for this kind of work, so I turned to my father, who had been a mid-level manager for most of his career and whose respect for people's humanity I admired. During my first year at the CWC, my father and I spent several evenings on the phone in hard conversations about how to treat the writing assistants with respect and flexibility, yet also help them to feel safe and to trust me by establishing consistent boundaries. With his guidance, and honest conversations with writing assistants, we created a discursive ecology in which we could draw from what we brought to the center and collaborate to create something new.

Just like the students in the Neighborhood Academic Initiative summer writing project, the writing assistants brought ever-branching networks of experience and relationships with them to the CWC. One was a mother of three young children, going to school and getting a divorce, whose phenomenal organizing abilities both kept her kids humming along in their lives and initiated administrative systems for the CWC. Another writing assistant from the CWC's early days wanted to partner with a particular drug detox program, but when I called the organization, they said they weren't interested. The writing assistant told me that I hadn't asked the right way, that I needed to know how to talk to the staff there—which he did, having been through the program himself. Rather than try to "mushfake" my way through another conversation with the program, I asked him to call, and within two days, he had set up a meeting with them—which turned into a six-month partnership for people undergoing their first few weeks of detox. One of the first writing assistants applied for the job not because he really liked writing but because it sounded "sort of interesting" and was placed at the CWC as a work-study student. When the CWC's slow start began to wear on his already limited interest, he revealed that he had always been interested in databases and wanted to create one to track the writers and projects for the center. We spent $75 for him to take a two-week course, and he developed, from scratch, a database system that we used for nearly five years. Writing assistants drew energies from their relationships to develop an art gallery dedicated to writing, to link the CWC to peace movements at the start of the Iraq War, and to link to the LDS church's employment training program, where we helped their volunteers improve their writing coaching strategies in their work with job seekers. The breadth of the CWC's relationships with the Salt Lake community was absolutely dependent on the many writing assistants (and volunteers) who traveled through its space.

The academy, at least in the humanities, tends to construct knowledge as an individual commodity; in the environment of the Community Writing Center, knowledge making evolved into a shared activity based in rhetoric—a cooperative, rather than transfer of, discursive energy. As a result, ownership was also shared, and "not knowing" transformed from individual frustration into the potential for collaborative discovery. Writing assistant Rachel Meads remembered, "My best moments [were] when I [got] caught in writing coaching sessions or in workshops and I [didn't] know the answer . . . because then we [had] to find the answer together." It was not uncommon for a writing assistant to suddenly stop a coaching session, call for someone else to join in, and then eventually fill the center with conversation with the writer on his or her particular task. This kind of collaborative exchange differs, if subtly, from writing center efforts to turn academic hierarchies on their head by locating authority in the student tutor. In such situations, directors who value tutor knowledge and ability won't "interfere[e] in a difficult tutoring session" (Mattison 101). That's fair enough, and I'm sure Meads wouldn't have approved another writing assistant or me butting into a coaching session without request. However, the slight difference is a construct of expertise as an act of relationship—of discursive exchange—rather than something that a tutor acquires through instruction and experience. Similar to coaching sessions, workshop facilitators (not subject to institutional measurements of success) were encouraged to let go of the notion that they had to "teach" the participants. Instead, the goal was to create a temporary learning space that transformed over the course of mere hours or weeks based on the relationships of the travelers therein. In fact, Shannon Bell said that she "knew [a workshop] was going really well" when the participants started to take over and remake the curriculum she had prepared.

This developing ease with uncertainty, with welcoming the unknown, contributed to the CWC's rhetoric of respect (and also would inform the CWC's relationship with community partners). Because the writing assistants and I were traveling organisms—with rhetorical capacities and vast experience in critical thinking beyond our academic credentials—joined together in an unstable environment, we related to one another as collaborative problem solvers. Meads's favorite response to a question from a writer, "I have no idea; let's figure it out," just might describe the discursive ecology of the Community Writing Center—a comfort with not-knowing mixed with confidence in potential resolution through collaboration. A further effect of the CWC's collaborative environment was that it opened space in which to take risks; by disconnecting expertise (and thus ownership) from the individual, the fear of "losing face" or failure was reduced dramatically, allowing us to try new things and to fail together.

And a lot of failure took place at the Community Writing Center, even as it moved toward sustainability. In the next chapter, I detail several of these failures and how they became catalysts for change. Here, though, I'd like to remember one of our biggest collective mistakes, when the writing assistants and I completely misread the potential of a particular time and particular place.

In February 2002, just five short months after the CWC opened its doors to the public, the Winter Olympics came to Salt Lake City. Some writing assistants were caught up in "Olympic fever," while others could take it or leave it. (I was in the latter category and left for a two-week vacation since the city's higher education institutions closed for the games.) Even so, when we discovered that the main visitor "disgorging" site for the buses transporting volunteers and spectators into the city was going to be just outside our front door, we marveled at our good fortune and opportunity. Thousands and thousands of people, from all over the state, country, the entire world!, would be passing by our front door. Surely the SLCC Community Writing Center could play a meaningful role in the Olympic experience—and phenomenally increase our local, national, and even global exposure.

The writing assistants went into action, brainstorming ways to tie writing into the Olympic theme, "Light the Fire Within!," eventually agreeing on the hokey yet, we hoped, mass-appealing "Light Your Writer Within!" We imagined being overrun by hordes of people who wanted to put their Olympic experience into words, either for their own memories or to share with others. Before the Games arrived, Sara Gunderson and Stephanie McKee painted "Welcome" in twenty-five different languages all across the CWC's front windows and plastered posters all over the area inviting people to "Don't just trade pins! Trade Experiences!"[17]

The Olympics began. Two writing assistants and I left town for our respective faraway places while the others stayed put, brimming with excitement for the onslaught of traded Olympic experiences. Two weeks later I parked my car at the CWC on my way to the closing ceremony parties in downtown Salt Lake. As I passed by the center, I noticed that it was dark, with doors closed and no sign of activity. I particularly noticed the absence of any "Light Your Writer Within!" paraphernalia; we had imagined pasting the written stories on the windows and walls of the center. "Hmm," I said to my husband and friends, "maybe it didn't go so well." The next morning I got to the CWC at 9:00 a.m. and saw Stephanie and another writing assistant sitting on the couch, looking depressed. "How'd it go?" I asked. "It completely sucked," they said in unison. "Really? So, not that many people came in?" Stephanie snarled, "No, not *that* many. Actually, not a single person came in." I couldn't believe it, not a single person out of the thousands of people walking by came into the CWC during those two weeks. "Maybe we didn't write 'Welcome' big enough?" I teased them.

Collaboratively, we had failed. We had completely overestimated the appeal of writing and the desire to document experience while it was happening. We forgot about needing space and time to reflect on experience and room to decide how to present it. (We had also underestimated the amount of alcohol that spectators would consume; a few inebriated people did come in looking for a bathroom.) By trying to turn the center into a meaningful part of the Olympics in Salt Lake, we overlooked the chance to easily promote the Community Writing Center simply by passing out small cards or leaflets. That failure contributed to our humility, to the awareness that we didn't know what the community wanted, that the small group of people who made up the CWC needed to rely on the relationships that we had—or would build—with others outside of the center if we were to survive.

⌒

I'd like to end this chapter by returning to Alisabeth McQueen, who said she was terrified by the opportunity to define her own writing assistant identity. When she facilitated her first writing workshop at the CWC, she was of course scared. Later, though, I heard through the writing assistant grapevine how angry she was that we expected her to do it. She wasn't a teacher and wasn't a writer; how could we put her in that situation—setting her up for failure? McQueen was hugely relieved when the workshop cancelled due to low enrollment, but she was faced with another one, and then another, that she collaboratively developed with other writing assistants and then shared with the workshop participants. Her comfort with uncertainty grew, as did her trust in the collaborative expertise at the CWC.

About a year after McQueen started, the SLCC English department asked if the CWC could provide an introduction to desktop publishing for faculty in their new Publication Center because they knew we had done a lot of inhouse publishing projects. When McQueen, who was then the website and marketing guru at the center, was asked to do it, her initial response was "no way," especially because one or two of the faculty she would be teaching had been her own composition instructors. With a little coaxing, and assurances of collaborating on the preparation, she did it. The faculty loved her presentation, and the department invited her back a few months later for a follow-up workshop. When I asked her if she was nervous, she said, "Oh, no, it won't be a problem. I just hope that they pay attention better than they did last time. You know, faculty aren't very good at being students, are they?" I had to smile and agree that no, faculty aren't the best students. They're too used to being the experts.

4

Shifting Relations, Transforming Expectations

"Can the CWC show me how to do a résumé that will get me a job?"
"We can help with your writing, but the rest is pretty much out of our hands."

"Can the CWC collect people's stories for our community empowerment project?"
"Yes, if they want to share them."

"Has the CWC made a difference in SLCC's enrollment?"
"We don't really know."
"Then how can you say the CWC has made a change?"
"Look at everyone who writes; . . . tell us that's not change."

In Chapter 3, I investigated discursive exchanges between the organisms inside the Community Writing Center. In this chapter, I focus on the CWC as an organism itself, one in relationship with others in the larger environment of Salt Lake City. While founding the CWC, Stephen Ruffus and I believed the center would relate to the community by providing accessible and flexible learning opportunities that would empower individuals and local organizations to address problems and reach goals. Using salvific discourse, the first catchphrase of the Community Writing Center was, "Writing opens minds, builds bridges, and improves lives." At that time, our intentions could have been subjected to Jeff Grabill's critique of academic assumptions that community-based work is inevitably empowering for the people who participate in it (117). Moreover, our approach was the kind that Linda Flower cautioned against in an email exchange with me: collaborations are too often measured on how close the community partner's participation fits within an educational version of what it means to "change."[1] Unfortunately, being aware of this troublesome notion of empowerment does not necessarily eliminate its influence over the meaning of such work, particularly for academic practitioners. Even after my decade spent in the community, academic notions of empowerment still affected how I interpreted what might be considered "change."

In 2010, a handful of months after I left the Community Writing Center, I returned to the center for a reading event jointly sponsored by the CWC and a center for homeless youth in Salt Lake City. The partnership—a writing group for the youth—had started a year earlier, and I was excited to listen to what they had written. Because of the uncertainties that youth living on the streets face, participation in the weekly group was sporadic, though the youth center valued the stability of a time and place for youth to write. Writers dropped in from time to time, maybe returning the next week, maybe not. Because of this, the CWC facilitator, Ken Simin, favored writing activities that focused on what could be produced in the moment rather than spending time on revision. In that particular relationship space, writing was a temporary activity, not a long-term commitment.

Just after 6:00 p.m., about a dozen people milled around inside the CWC, chatting with the kind of lively intimacy shared by close groups. A few of them were youth who had participated in the writing workshop, the others center staff and volunteers. Loud laughter punctuated the pockets of conversation around the room as we waited for other writers to walk the mile or so from a free health clinic program they were attending. About an hour had passed when they came through the door, shed their many layers of coats, and dropped themselves into the rows of seats.

The performance started with a young woman singing a song she had written just that morning. Accompanying herself on guitar, she sang of "karma coming to get" those who had hurt her and that she would stay strong. Next, a young man read a poem he had written about chaos. A young woman who followed wanted to sing a Mary J. Blige song but couldn't get up the nerve to do so and switched to an impromptu monologue about how thankful she was to the youth center for helping her "get and stay clean" and for being her "real family." Then a young man slouching in the corner stood up, grabbed the microphone, and began an angry stand-up comedy routine that criticized his biological family, the youth center staff, and several of the other youth in the room. A young woman following him said that she wanted to show some pictures she had taken but didn't have a computer. A writing assistant went in search of a laptop while another young woman stepped up and declared that she wanted to become politically active—and a voice for the kids on the street—and then read a poem about "streeters" (street kids). After that, a young man told some jokes, and he was followed by more songs, poems, and impromptu expressions of gratitude for the youth center.

Later that evening, I thought about what Eli Goldblatt had written in *Because We Live Here*. In the final chapter, Goldblatt presented the SLCC Community Writing Center in a promising light but at the same time questioned the long-term value of the CWC's DiverseCity Writing Series (DWS) program, partially due to its emphasis on writing group autonomy. I had written previously about the changes the DWS program had made since its inception:

> [The program] appears to be emerging as its own set of multiple discourse communities, supported, but not constructed, by an educational institutional paradigm. Each writing group is developing its own identity and style of interaction, while at the same time remaining a part of the matrix of groups within the larger program. (Rousculp, "When the Community" 78)

In response, Goldblatt praised the idea of the DWS program yet also wrote, "We want to avoid being exploitive and co-opting in the way we package and gloss community-based writing, but beyond the first exhilaration of hearing their stories read in public and appear in print, what do new authors get for their involvement in a non-interventional press sponsored by the academy?" (199). Even though I knew that most of the community writers got a lot more out of the DWS than Goldblatt might have imagined,[2] his question troubled how I experienced the youth reading event that evening.

The partnership between the CWC and the youth center was quite "noninterventional": writers dropped in and out, wrote what they wanted or didn't, and then at the performance did pretty much anything they wanted, very little of which came from the writing group's time. Later I learned that the evening had been presented to the youth as an open-mic event at which any kind of expression was welcome, which made the range of performances more understandable. And the evening was pleasant and fun; the youth laughed a lot and appeared to have a good time. However, I still wondered how the CWC's resources were contributing to the youths' "change" or "empowerment"; the performances didn't seem to demonstrate how their yearlong partnership with the CWC had made any difference in their lives, nor produced much writing. (And I wondered: if an SLCC administrator had been there, would he or she have asked the same question—accompanied by concerns about how college money was being spent?)

As I discussed in the previous chapter, educators survive and thrive by adapting to environments that privilege individual knowledge. As such, they may tend to subconsciously (or consciously) position themselves as possessing a clear understanding of the priorities of community partners, who are then constructed as needing academic resources to improve their life conditions. Relationships evolve in which the academic partner is allowed to identify as "whole" while the community partner is assumed to be "broken" or "not-quite-whole" and in need of specific change. Even though I had been sensitized to this kind of relationship, I still fell into a disrespectful interpretation of the youth reading event by weaving an ideological web around what constituted change. Because of this, the most "change-like" moment of the evening for me took place when two of the youth registered with the CWC and signed up for writing coaching sessions the following week. I recognized this kind of change: participating in educational opportunities to empower oneself. But in doing so, I defined these young men as being in need of a specific revision. In other words, I measured them by how far they wanted to migrate into my environment. My interpretation required them to transgress their current identities rather than for me to pay attention to my own. As Paula Mathieu warns in her book *Tactics of Hope*, such academic measurements of community partnership outcomes risk replication of the hegemony that higher education already holds over the larger community. I knew this—and still fell right into this way of thinking.

In this chapter, I map webs of relationships that the Community Writing Center traversed with other organisms for twelve years and how those relationships altered the CWC's understanding of "change." In doing so, I trace how the CWC positioned itself in relation to its partners, how it developed a nuanced sense of what change was, and how it transformed away from a rhetoric of "liberatory" education into a rhetoric of respect for the priorities and ideologies of the people and organizations we collaborated with. Perhaps unexpectedly, given the transformation from an individual to a collective understanding of knowledge making within the Community Writing Center (as the previous chapter demonstrates), our understanding of change for our partners took a different—though not opposite—turn. Specifically, "change" became defined for the CWC not as collective action or anticipated outcome but as the potential for individuals to use writing as they see fit, to exercise agency over textual production within regulatory systems in ways they deem most appropriate for themselves at a particular moment in their lives.

LOOKING OUT FROM INSIDE HIGHER EDUCATION

When Ruffus and I were making proposals to SLCC administrators about the Community Writing Center, we had to establish a need for the project, a need that indicated a lack of resources in the community that were (a) not already being met and (b) important to the mission of Salt Lake Community College. Just like any government agency or philanthropic foundation, SLCC administrators directed funding toward their priorities and to where their resources could make a significant—or publicly recognized—change in the community. To persuade them, we had to construct the community as "not quite whole" and in need of a college-sponsored center that would make them whole. In early documents, written in the spring of 2000, we documented evidence that 60 percent of Salt Lake County residents experienced "significant impairments in their literacy abilities." We also used data to argue that only "10% of needy adults receive required services" and "residents who do have basic skills . . . are overlooked in the scramble to address the 'literacy crisis'" (Rousculp, "SLCC Community" 16). In response to such needs, we claimed that

> utilizing a drop-in writing center and several community out-reach writing programs, the SLCC Community Writing Center (CWC) will serve people who are prevented from achieving individual success and participating in their communities. These people struggle with limited literacy abilities, lack of confidence and, sometimes, cultural and/or economic barriers. The CWC resources and programs will empower these people in their own lives and will enrich the life of the Salt Lake community.

Such need-based discourse—"prevented from," "struggle," "limited," "lack"—is common to funding requests regardless of how the applicant might actually feel about those they are proposing to support, and so it is not proposal discourse that I am concerned with. Instead, I am interested in how those making such a proposal navigate the web from envisioned proposal to actual relationship. Does the textual attitude that necessarily informs proposals carry forward into the community writing partnership, or does it pivot into one that respects partners as whole and complex persons?

Though we had to use need-based discourse in proposals, the principles that grounded the CWC tried to disrupt the oft-practiced model of importing expertise and resources into a needy community. At the same time, we believed that higher education, particularly publicly funded higher education, had an obligation to share its assets in order to contribute to the overall health of surrounding communities. Although we knew that higher education partnerships could be fraught with exploitation and cynicism, we hoped that the community college environment (as opposed to that of a research institution)[3] from which we engaged with the community would lead to relationships based on collaboration rather than need and expertise.

Still, as I have described, it took us a while to get there (and even when we did, we were not always consistent about it). Even though early CWC documents indicate the beginning of a rhetoric of respect, they also clearly show how we imagined our project as somehow "different" from the community by using inside/outside metaphors common to higher education partnerships. Initially, we defined the center as an "outreach project of the SLCC Writing Program" without troubling boundaries implied by "outreach." Though not quite the import/export model that Susan Miller wanted to resist, the outreach metaphor illustrated that the CWC's purpose was to offer something to the community but not become a part of it. We wanted *to provide* educational access to people who didn't have it and we wanted *to give* voice to those who were not heard. In doing so, we nearly always positioned the CWC as "whole" and imagined the community as "not-quite-whole"—and, of course, grateful—recipients. Though we didn't intend to do so, such need-based discourse transcended our funding proposals and found its way into how we originally constructed relationships between the CWC and organizations in the community.

When the Community Writing Center opened, we made a lot of cold calls to different organizations to introduce ourselves. Many organizations were unsure what a community writing center was (as were we!), but most expressed a desire (or as, we characterized it then, a "need") for writing instruction specifically tailored to their employees, volunteers, and clients. Some organizations wanted their staff and clients to get involved in the civic sphere, others wanted to provide creative "team building" writing activities. Nearly all said that at least one of their employees "couldn't write" and or had "really bad grammar." Imagining an onslaught of projects, the writing assistants and I established a process to sort through and prioritize them. This process included an application form that asked organizations to make a case for why the Community Writing Center should take them on as a partner, specifically addressing how their proposal reflected the CWC's mission and its potential for sustainability. Our hubris resulted in a five-page application packet, of which I provide a small sample:

The Community Writing Center accepts applications for Writing Project Partnerships from community organizations, non-profits, and for-profit organizations. The Community Writing Center provides a variety of resources to an organization working on a specific project that involves written communication and believes that "quality education should provide alternative and on-going learning opportunities to the communities it serves and individuals and organizations should be active participants in the education of their communities." Because the goal of these project partnerships is the eventual self-sufficiency of the applicant, a human resources contribution is necessary to acceptance of the applications.

Applications will be reviewed twice a year, in June and November. The number of partnerships each cycle will be based on the resources and capacity of the CWC.

On the surface, the application seems to adhere to common elements of proposals: boundaries and expectations, deadlines and criteria. Yet a decade on from it, it is embarrassing to remember that we tried to work with organizations in this way. We presumed that organizations would agree to organize their requests around our biannual schedule and would accept the CWC (an unknown entity at that point) adjudicating their worthiness. Additionally, we implied that with the CWC's help, a partner could gain "eventual self-sufficiency" (as if they weren't already self-sufficient). Further, because we wanted to engage in partnerships, not service work, we required that education be a focus for the organization (which it might not have been), and also that they dedicate "human resources" to contribute to a partnership (not to mention just to complete the extensive application).

Certainly, a partnership with shared educational goals, mutual human effort and resource contribution, and a strong sense of collaborative ownership is something to aspire to. Some of the best CWC partnerships included aspects of such reciprocity, even though the ideal didn't necessarily line up with the day-to-day realities of such work. Ralph Cintron critiques the "automatic virtue" of such admired goals as "democracy" and "inclusion" under which well-intentioned projects may ignore the "material limitation[s]" they may be contending with (103). He writes that "social contract models," in which I would include collaboration and reciprocity, "traditionally ignore material resources" (106). We had done just this when we ignored one of the primary reasons that organizations might seek assistance on a project: lack of sufficient resources to enact it, or even to identify what it might be (beyond "improving bad writing").

Not realizing how badly we had configured our relationship with potential partners, we released the application with excitement, sending it out to dozens of community organizations that had expressed interest in working with us. While we waited for submissions to fill our inbox, we talked about how we would sort through the proposals and worried about how we would meet all of the requests. And we waited. And waited.

Nothing happened. Not a single proposal came in. Not even from the organizations that talked with us enthusiastically about working together. And rightly so. As Stephen Parks writes in *Gravyland*, "Once I made the move to turn theories into practice, I quickly learned the value of humility" (xxxi). The organizations' silence was reminiscent of how community leaders had responded to me in the Artspace Bridge Project negotiations: a young teacher out of her league, as the nascent CWC was out of its league. The center at that point was a fledgling organism (maybe a tadpole?) trying to figure out what it was or what it would be, and in doing so, we made inaccurate assumptions about its worth—about writing's worth—to different communities. Even worse, we had positioned the CWC as a resource superior to potential partners, not recognizing that we needed their resources to reach our own goals as much, if not more, than they needed us to reach theirs. In this failure, we had to recognize the Community Writing Center as a single entity moving along a much larger web of community and governmental agencies and activist and regulatory groups, and that we had created the CWC not only to help them achieve their goals but also to achieve our own.

Regardless of their stability or size, organizations have agency; by ignoring the CWC's Writing Partner application process, community organizations changed how the CWC would approach relationships. The CWC could not dictate to partners a set of learning methods or outcomes if it hoped to sustain itself. We soon discovered that individual community members likewise exerted their agency in relationship with the center, which led to transformed definitions of what education, and thus change, could be.

Inside educational environments, teachers set learning and performance goals for students based on curricula designed by academic departments and approved by educational institutions (and statewide and national bodies). Students submit to requirements and evaluations because these are the institutionally mandated pathways toward their certification as educated persons. When learning moves outside of these regulatory structures, however, the relationship between learner and teacher can dramatically shift: learners can determine the course of their experience. The year after the CWC opened, we received a small grant from the local humanities council to conduct a "Family Folklore" workshop led by two academically trained folklorists, Dru Hazleton, a faculty member at the college, and Michael Christensen, a professional folklorist for the Utah Cultural Celebration Center in West Valley City (adjacent to the Taylorsville/Kearns area). Hazleton and Christensen created a curriculum that instructed participants in data collection techniques and interpretation strategies to render written documents suitable for archival purposes. After their second meeting (of nine), Hazleton and Christensen came to me very frustrated because they "couldn't get the participants to do folklore." Rather than following discipline-approved techniques of gathering, documenting, and interpreting their data, participants were "just telling stories." By this time, I had had several experiences of a workshop changing course midway. Just as Shannon Bell said that she knew a workshop was going well when the participants took over, I congratulated the folklorists and suggested that if the writers were telling stories, then the workshop wasn't about folklore anymore. I asked if they could instead work with the writers to create new types of research and text production that were informed by elements of folklore. This pushed too hard against their disciplinary range of tolerance; they believed they could get the group "back on track" the following week.

A week later, Hazleton and Christensen said, "It didn't work, they're still telling stories . . . but they're really pretty good stories." Absent the regulations that allow teachers and administrators to define when learning or change happens, the community writers altered the meaning of the workshop and created what they wanted it to be. They wrote personal narratives, family histories, bilingual legends, and "true detective" histories of their ancestors. They used folkloric and historical approaches that created hybrid writing genres that were meaningful to them.

⌒

For just a moment, I need to follow a different strand to address the elephant in the room: funding and accountability—both issues fundamental to survival and sustainability. It is not unusual for educational and community programs to be held captive to decontextualized assessments dictated by funding agencies (philanthropic or government). For example, a long-term partner of the Community Writing Center, the Literacy Action Center, faced federal funding dependent upon improvement in their learners' scores on the Test for Adult Basic Education (TABE). While they documented that their learners showed significant increases in how they engaged with texts in their daily lives, they struggled to show improvement on this exam.[4]

In the case of the folklore writing workshop, the money was granted to the CWC for a specific purpose. Although community participants altered that purpose, the funding remained intact. Does this mean the Community Writing Center was treated differently by its funding agencies (specifically, by the college) than other programs might have been? I don't think it was. On the contrary, the CWC prioritized accountability for both external (grant-based) and internal (college-based) funding. For external funding, the center provided assessment for each grant it received just as any other organization would. For the folklore workshop, the narrative report recognized that there were "some challenges merging scholarship with presentation." It also noted as a "weakness" of the project, "Emphasis on archiving materials and documentation seemed to take a back seat as projects moved forward." Even so, we were also able to report, "Participants presented a variety of stories and analyses that we were able to classify and introduce thematically. . . . From Carbon County miners and Chicago policemen (which merged family stories and occupational folklore) to Depression era narratives and names (which resulted in an identity theme), both workshop participants and audience members got a good representation of themes." The humanities council was completely satisfied with the project and invited the CWC to apply for a similar grant the following funding cycle.

In terms of the primary funder of the CWC, the community college, the center was subject to evaluative tools similar to those used to evaluate the rest of the college's departments and programs. Always cognizant of our vulnerability in the overall funding picture, we strove to stay ahead of the assessment curve by consistently evaluating our work and reporting results to college administration. We provided them with our strategic plans and annual objectives, as well as quarterly reports of quantitative and qualitative evidence of the program's activities. In 2003, just shy of the first budget crisis that nearly closed the CWC, the center participated in the college's national accreditation report, aligning three intended outcomes with the stated college goals, collecting data, and reporting on the results. One particular outcome, "By respecting and encouraging diversity, and with a commitment to creating a community of learners through dynamic and innovative learning opportunities, the CWC will provide useful writing assistance and workshops to a broad variety of individuals in the Salt Lake community," was evaluated through the demographics of Writer Registration forms and a simple survey sent to writers who used the center. The results indicated that "in every race/ethnic category, the CWC [writer demographics] exceeded the diversity of Salt Lake City," and survey responses indicated that the "CWC provided useful writing assistance and resources." Over the years I was at the CWC, protocol became more formalized, but the flexible assessment environment of higher education—as compared to public education—allowed the CWC to work with the Institutional Assessment Office to develop meaningful and reliable data for the college. The time I had spent working with the Development Office while crafting the initial proposals for the center allowed me to adapt my discourses to those that would demonstrate the financial worth of the Community Writing Center to the college.[5]

↜

The realization that the CWC could not determine the methods or outcomes of the projects it facilitated was central to the evolution of how the Community Writing Center engaged with partners. We discarded the Writing Partner application process and tended relationships that we already had. As I mentioned in the previous chapter, a writing assistant who had undergone detox himself made the connection with the drug recovery program. A friend of mine who directed a county health program asked the CWC to provide writing coaching for her staff as they worked through public information documents. Workshops sprouted at previous DiverseCity Writing Series locations. We also paid close attention to our habits of conversation, specifically developing our ability to listen. Our changed approach appeared to work. Six months after opening, our mid-year report noted that we had made connections with "nearly 150 agencies and organizations" and that we had "established a strong relationship with the Salt Lake City Library," which had become "our #1 referral site." Four months after that, we were able to report to the SLCC president that "we predicted that 200 individuals would register as writers with the CWC by the end of the summer; we have 300 people signed up so far. We wanted to hold at least four workshops for the public; we have already held seven for the public and have run nearly 20 in collaboration with community organizations."

As the CWC became a more recognizable presence in the Salt Lake community, we never went back to an application process for partnerships. Very occasionally an organization requested a formal memorandum of understanding (MOU) for funding purposes, or a particularly complex partnership might have included documentation of which partner was responsible for certain elements of a collaboration. As the CWC pivoted on its particular intersection of the webs of education and community, we developed partnerships through conversation and building relationships with the community, not by asserting our essentialness to it.[6]

WHAT CHANGE LOOKS LIKE

Part of the Community Writing Center's clumsy negotiation of relationships stemmed from our higher education discursive ecologies. In retrospect, perhaps we should have been more aware of this. Another mistake we didn't see coming, however (and probably wouldn't have without going through it), was how our intention to improve the lives of others upset what could have been productive and reciprocal relationships. Surely, wanting one's work to have an impact is laudable, and the desire to do so infuses the goals of student writing centers, activist teacher-scholars, and, for that matter, anyone who hopes to contribute their efforts to disrupt social and economic inequities. In community literacy work, seeking change is ubiquitous, as noted by Elenore Long: "The goal of leveraging institutional resources to bring about progressive social change is generally shared across community-literacy scholars" (4). It is hard to argue against efforts that challenge oppression, empower people to act, provide access to learning, or reduce social ills. There are many ways to go about such work; in the SLCC Community Writing Center's case, we hoped to do so within a rhetoric of respect and in collaboration with others. Over time, however, we realized that even though we were collaborative in our intentions, we were actually seeking a particular kind of change—the "right" kind of change.

One bias that cultivated the Community Writing Center's early vision of change was the centrality of civic engagement to the discipline of rhetoric, both historically and in its more recent "public turns" (Mathieu; Flower [*Community*, "Going Public"]; George and Mathieu; Ackerman and Coogan).[7] Within rhetoric, "'civic' is a keyword . . . as it is synonymous with 'city' . . . and is synonymic with 'civility,'" with a commitment to "consensual discourse" (Ackerman 76). Accordingly, engaging community members through civic writing was a driving force from the beginning of the CWC, articulated in an early mission statement this way: "Successful urban communities have thoughtful conversations about social and economic quality, acceptance of diversity, and peaceful relations AND Thoughtful writing for others is one important way to promote these conversations" (see Appendix B).[8] Toward this goal, early CWC documents stated intentions to partner with two organizations also planning to move into the Artspace Bridge Projects, an antiracism nonprofit and a community mediation startup, in order to nurture intercultural think tanks like those that Peck, Flower, and Higgins developed at the Community Literacy Center (CLC). When these partnerships didn't pan out, we tapped into the energy of the city's "Bridging the Religious Divide" initiative and facilitated a micro-version of the CLC think-tank process.

In preparation, Ron Christiansen, an SLCC English department faculty member and an intellectually critical member of the LDS church, researched the rivaling process developed through the CLC in which participants actively seek out alternative perspectives and hypotheses on a sociocultural, sociopolitical issue.[9] Christiansen created a special project called "Belief(s) in SLC: Writing through Differences" to address the following:

> Salt Lake City has a long history of misunderstanding between the majority LDS religion and other minority positions within the community. While many individuals and groups have successfully initiated dialogue and conversation through panels and speakers, it seems difficult at best to fully address the underlying contexts and values that inform the views of each side.

Participants in the project came from both LDS backgrounds and non-LDS backgrounds (with a wide range of emotional connections to the faith) and had "candid discussions about some of the issues that divide the SLC community: gay marriage, stereotyping, the purpose of religion, and the belief in an afterlife." They also produced dozens of short writings during the three months of the project. Despite great effort, however, the group was not able to develop the "hybrid discourses" that emerged from the CLC rivaling projects, where seemingly polarized perspectives could be articulated in mutually affirming ways. As Christiansen wrote, "it proved hard, as [he had] anticipated, to keep LDS people involved." Out of the five active LDS members who started out, only one stayed throughout the project, but did not submit a final piece of writing. When there was "nowhere to go" for someone because of their religious beliefs, individuals removed themselves from the conversation because they had "little to gain, and possibly much to lose." Christiansen concluded that "this ties into the age old question of how to motivate those in power to interrogate their positions and possible abuses of this power, especially when their participation may put them in difficult, uncomfortable or threatening situations. It proved difficult at best." Christiansen had told me that he thought a rivaling process would be extremely difficult for active LDS members to engage in, but he was willing to try a new approach to getting at the divide in the city to support the CWC's commitment to civic engagement.

Despite this commitment to balancing our efforts toward personal, practical, and civic purposes, we were dedicated to collaboratively evolving the CWC's programs with the community. This collaborative stance resulted in many more personal and practical writing projects than those engaging with the civic sphere. Sometimes it seemed as though civic writing projects were initiated only by the Community Writing Center, never by the public or by partner organizations. Over time, we became concerned that if the public only wanted to write stories and résumés, the CWC might turn into a type of writing salon–emergency aid station in which people would gather in their spare time to share their personal memories or work frantically with a writing coach on an application that would finally land them a job. This worry led to the development of what I might call a "civic addiction." Symptoms included desperately seeking any sign of civic engagement at the Community

Writing Center, hanging onto moments when writers showed signs of wanting to challenge or question inequality. I didn't realize just how much this infused my relationship with the Community Writing Center's writers until one evening during a DiverseCity Writing Series public reading event.

As with most DWS reading events, it was an emotional gathering of writing, people, and community, celebrating the program's eighth anthology publication, *So They Said*. Twenty writers from a wide range of backgrounds and writing groups shared stories of love, loss, family, dreams, fantasy, and fiction. Some of the readers were from a DWS writing group that partnered the CWC with the Literacy Action Center (LAC), a literacy organization working with adult native English speakers—"nonreaders" and "beginning readers"—who used their own stories to learn to read. Some writers dictated to a tutor and then practiced reading what they had said, while others wrote what they could. At DWS events, LAC writers were marked by their slow and determined reading voices, occasionally stopping for assistance on a particular word, and receiving the most praise for their effort and bravery as they shared their words with a public audience.

Most often, writers from the LAC read short personal stories about themselves or members of their families—sometimes a paragraph or two, sometimes a couple of pages—but that night, Terry Trigger, a man in his mid-fifties, stood up, walked to the center of the stage, and read "President Bush, Stop Killing Our Families!"

I am asking the President of the United States and the senators to stop the war!!! I am tired of our boys and girls being blown up in cars and buses and at dinner. The deaths are senseless. Our sons and daughters need a fair chance to have a real life of their own. Many of them have babies and spouses, but these soldiers are dead. The spouses and children have to go on without their partners or parents. Moms and dads have to go on without their sons and daughters.

My son was in the war in 2003. He was sent home because he was shot. I think all of our people should come home because I really don't feel this is our war! It is really Saddam Hussein's war with his people. He was the ruler of his people, killing them for no reason. His people wished that he was destroyed. Are we still in this war because we haven't found Osama bin Laden?

I feel for the good Iraqi men, women, and children, but the bad people—the ones who are shooting our troops—should get what they get. I wouldn't want our U.S. to be like their country. Wouldn't it be nice if our countries could be like sisters and brothers? If we could continue helping Iraq with food and finances after our troops are out, maybe they will stop fighting and build their country back even better than before! (54)

When he finished, I burst into loud applause with the rest of the audience. Trigger's words gave me a momentary "hit" for my civic addiction, and the fact that it came from a man with low literacy skills made the moment even more satisfying. The voiceless had spoken, the silenced had been heard. At the CWC reception for the readers, I made a point to tell Trigger how great I thought his piece was and that I was moved by his courage. He smiled and said thank you.

A few days later, as I was looking through an earlier DiverseCity Writing Series publication, *There Is a Shorter View*, I came across another of Trigger's contributions, a letter to his wife/partner, "To You, Dear."

I know that you are the only one in my life. I want to be with you for the rest of my life.

You are the only one that makes me happy. I have been in love with you from the day that I met you.

This is the first letter I have ever written to you. I hope you understand why I didn't write one to you before. I have never written to anybody because I didn't know how to spell or read.

We've been together for 18 years. We have had our ups and down. But no matter what has happened in our lives, I've always been with you.

> Dear, you know that you have always made me happy.
> I'm sorry that I haven't worked for the last three years. I am
> going back to school to get a job, then I can get back to work.
> (11)

I remembered the night that Trigger read this piece, two years earlier. I had noticed the vulnerability he had expressed and was moved, but I did not experience the same "high" as when he spoke out politically. As I reread his letter, I realized that I had imposed my own measure of what change was on Trigger's writing, rather than recognizing him as a whole person whose priorities were more important than those I imagined for him—and for the Community Writing Center. When I talked to Trigger in an interview for this book, I asked what he felt when he wrote the two pieces. He said they were just completely different from each other. The letter to his partner came from a place that was "locked up inside" him that he could only explain through writing. He then said he wrote the political letter because he was angry and frustrated about the war, feeling as though it had become a pointless exercise that only led to pointless deaths. We talked about how it felt futile to try to change our politicians' minds and actions, and then he ended our conversation with, "But, what are you gonna do? I don't know what's going to happen." Afterward, I spoke with the director of the Literacy Action Center, Deborah Young, about my interpretation of Trigger's writing. When I asked her if she thought he felt more empowered by one or the other, she replied, "I don't think he sees his writing as empowering; that's an academic interpretation of what he is doing. He just wanted to get his voice out there to be heard about things that were important to him."

An academic interpretation. Looking out from an academic web, we seek to change discourses that maintain or promote oppression—from the luxurious standpoint of not being directly subjected to them. In doing so, we can overlook the perspectives of those we are advocating for. Dobrin and Weisser argue, "Social constructivist approaches often rely too heavily upon collectivist, cumulative perspectives and risk overlooking the individual's position and experience and how those are shaped through interaction with various environmental factors" (158). When I reacted to Trigger's different pieces of writing, I assigned them value based on my position as an activist teacher, not on how he experienced them as an individual.

So which path does a rhetoric of respect take? Toward the individual or toward the broader resistance of oppressive systems? At the CWC, negotiating respect for individual experience along with a commitment to the collective goal was a constant challenge. At times I thought that systemic change could take place through civic engagement, not through personal reflection and expression, though these types of writing experiences needed to be available to those who wanted them. One particular partnership, however, made transparent the potentially subtle exploitation of disenfranchised individuals by the very organizations that advocated on their behalf. In this particular situation, we had to make a choice between supporting the writers themselves or participating in their regulation.

We had been contacted by a small nonprofit organization that advocated politically for the rights of people with disabilities. In this partnership, the organization wanted to collect stories for a project called "Our Homes, Not Nursing Homes," which argued that people with disabilities should be able to use their federal support service benefits to live at home rather than in a nursing home or rehabilitation center. A participatory action researcher from the University of Utah was also involved in the project.

In initial meetings with the organization's staff and the university researcher, we learned that they wanted to use the workshop's resulting publication to "provide individuals living in nursing homes with more awareness of the choices they may have to move out of nursing homes and into community settings" and also "as a tool to lobby the state legislature" (Hayashi and Rousculp 62). As we discussed a possible curriculum, the organization's director emphasized that they needed written texts describing inhumane treatment experienced in nursing homes and rehabilitation centers. Stories of privacy invasion, humiliation, and chronic neglect swirled through their offices in daily conversation, though they needed to be documented to have a political impact. I and the writing assistant working on the project along with me agreed that it was a good fit for the CWC; the partnership seemed to be an opportunity to empower people personally and to collectively challenge the limits placed on them by society and, sometimes, by their own bodies.

The organization's director and the university researcher imagined that the participants would tell their stories to a CWC writing assistant, who would then revise them into advocacy narratives. Many of their clients couldn't physically write, and the organization didn't have the resources to acquire voice-recognition software. In response, we explained that the writers did the writing in CWC projects, and as much as we personally supported the organization's goals, reinterpreting the participants' words threatened to fall into bell hooks's critique:

> No need to hear your voice when I can talk about you better than you can speak about yourself. No need to hear your voice. Only tell me about your pain. I want to know your story. And, then I will tell it back to you in a new way. Tell it back to you in such a way that it has become mine, my own. Re-writing you as I write myself anew. I am still author, authority. I am still colonizer, the speaking subject, and you are now at the center of my talk. (151)

We explained that with collaborative support, we believed their clients could write their own stories. Together we agreed on a process in which participants would partner with volunteer "scribe-writing assistants," who would record and transcribe spoken stories. Following this, the writers would read the transcriptions in writing coaching sessions with the scribes and revise their work. Volunteers completed a truncated version of the CWC writing assistant training that familiarized them with collaborative writing processes, feedback, and revision strategies. In addition, they were expected to abide by the "Ethics of Writing Scribes" developed with the organization's director and university researcher.

> As writing scribes/assistants, you will serve a dual role in this project. Your writing assistant role will come into play as you

work with the writer to invent, draft, and revise his writing. You should pay attention to the Writing Assistant ethics and practices as you work with the writer.

However, the scribe role is more service-based in that you are providing a service (scribing) that the writer cannot physically do. In this role, you are the vehicle through which the writer expresses herself. You should remain very aware that your own interpretation, ideas, and expectations stay as far removed from the writer's composing process as possible.

For example, you will likely need to do some work in between our workshops getting your notes from the workshop organized or scribed to be able to use them the next week. At this point, it can be very tempting to interpret or organize based on your impression of how the writing "should" be. Resist this temptation to the best of your ability. Always remember that this is the writer's writing and while you will collaborate with her throughout the process, when you are scribing or compiling the writing, your purpose is to serve them, not to interpret.

After about two months of dividing up responsibilities, training volunteers, and developing the curriculum, we were ready to begin the four-week workshop. Eight participants, along with their scribes, gathered in the organization's warehouse office space. Some sat in chairs at a big table, while others sat to the side in mechanized wheelchairs. Oxygen pumps punctuated the silence with overlapping bursts of air. We handed out the schedule that began with invention, then drafting, and then finally high-order and low-order revision goals. (Though we knew the writers wouldn't follow a linear path through their writing, we hoped that drawing attention to writing processes might provide a scaffold for more hesitant writers.)

The first workshop started with the scribes recording and taking down notes as the writers talked. It quickly became apparent that the writers were not aware of what types of stories they were to tell. A few related stories about living in nursing homes, but several others wanted to write about their childhoods, or how and when they became disabled and how they coped. Even though the flier for the workshop clearly stated its purpose and what the writing would be used for—"to publish stories of people who survived living in nursing homes and those who want to live in the community and are waiting to get out" in order to "(1) Educate community leaders about the cost-effectiveness of community resources vs. nursing home care and (2) Provide examples and hope for people who want to leave nursing homes but need reassurance that they can be successful in the community"—these weren't the stories that were emerging.

It was clear that most of the writers were not "on task" with the project, and we weren't sure what to do. Did we align ourselves with the organization and redirect the participants' writing, or did we respect the choices of the individual writers? Since we didn't know if there had been a misunderstanding, during the second meeting the volunteers encouraged the writers to focus on their lives in nursing homes. Eventually writers began to talk and write about nursing homes and some revealed stories of neglect, sadness, and loss of control and dignity. Yet their stories were much more nuanced than it seemed the organization was anticipating. The writers displayed cogent awareness of the complexities of nursing homes and wrote of positive as well as negative experiences, such as enjoying activities provided to them and being "treated like a person" by certain administrators. They also acknowledged the "difficulties of working in a nursing home: '[They are] understaffed'" (Hayashi and Rousculp 63).

In addition to the personal relationships with people in the nursing homes in which they had lived or were still living, the writers were confronting a discursive problem that was quite different from their verbal venting, which took place in the safe environment of the advocacy organization: "One active member of the organization who was well-known for her frequent assertive complaints about the nursing home found it extremely difficult to put these concerns in writing, limiting herself to irritations resulting from a small bedroom, lack of privacy for her and her boyfriend, and being told what to do" (Hayashi and Rousculp 63). Though she had a history of detailing violations of dignity, privacy, and humane treatment, in her writing she came across as simply annoyed. Even though the project was intended to create a "counterpublic"[10] capable of speaking against the prevailing notions of people with disabilities, asking people to go public brought about unanticipated concerns. In an analysis of working with writers with disabilities, Linda Flower describes this conflict: "Celebrating the work of rhetoric from an enfranchised academic perspective [does] not always consider the difficulties going public might raise for others" ("Going Public" 137). For this group of writers, participating in the collective goal brought about distinct risks to their living conditions.[11]

Unfortunately, these outcomes frustrated the organization's director because she needed more concrete violations in order to carry out her advocacy work. She expressed her concerns to me and asked that the volunteers push for more stories that would be useful to the organization's objectives. At that point, however, it was clear that the writers understood how their stories were to be used, so we decided to respect their decisions about how to publicly present their stories. Perhaps because of this, the director decided to stop participating in the project and left it to the AmeriCorps VISTA member, who had originally contacted us about the project, to finish it up. In the end, we extended the workshop by two sessions and most of the writers completed their stories, but three volunteers dropped out due to the stressful environment.

In an academic article that the university researcher asked me to coauthor, we (predictably) interpreted the workshop in a positive light. We wrote, "It appears that this college–community partnership to empower members of a disadvantaged population was a success. All writers expressed positive feelings about having participated in the writing workshop. They realized that their life stories are worth telling and felt positive about their stories being used by [the advocacy organization] as organizing and lobbying tools" (Hayashi and Rousculp 67). The accuracy of this academic interpretation could be debated. But the experience informed how the Community Writing Center would interact with writers and partners in the future. We decided that in situations in which individual writers might not wish to adhere to an advocacy organization's purpose for their writing, we would not intervene on behalf of the organization. We would commit ourselves to a rhetoric of respect for the competent and whole individual and honor their choices and genres of writing. When this happened, the CWC diverged from a foundational principle that I had gained from Freire's work, that action must result from critical awareness, "and from that reflection will come [the oppressed's] necessary engagement in the struggle for liberation" (*Pedagogy of the Oppressed* 48). The Community Writing Center might try to make it possible for writers to struggle for liberation, but if the "oppressed" individual chose to do something else, that was what we respected.

There is an important point to make about our decision to align more closely with the individual than the organization. Some may interpret this as a romantic remnant of expressivist and process pedagogies in composition that have long been critiqued by social constructivist and postprocess scholars as ignoring sociocultural and sociopolitical contexts in which writing is produced and consumed. Further, it might be argued that prioritizing the individual is decidedly not an ecological approach, given that the "First Law of Ecology" is "everything is connected to everything else" (Commoner 16). An individual organism is but one small part of a much larger web of relationships and contexts. However, our decision to prioritize the writers with disabilities—and all subsequent individual writers—was in fact in response to the contexts (the web) in which they existed. The writers with disabilities had to contend with lives regulated by policies and restrictions in the nursing homes, the advocacy organization's objectives, and social classification of themselves as incomplete persons. But when space was made for them to speak/write what they chose, change could happen in ways that we might not have anticipated, nor might these changes have been recognizable through the lens of liberatory pedagogies.

Ellen Cushman's *The Struggle and the Tools* argues that liberatory terms of defining change are out of touch with the realities of people whom such pedagogies propose to empower:

If critical consciousness leads to collective action, the instances presented in this book simply will not live up to this standard. But the problem here isn't with the community members' lack of political awareness and savvy—the problem is with this definition. This . . . definition fails to reflect social realities where critical consciousness does not always lead to collective action nor to unified class struggle. (xx)

Removing "collective" from the tolerances of critical consciousness opens up resistance and empowerment to include individual acts in which we can "begin to appreciate how individuals can both accommodate and undermine, both placate and rebuff, both obey and challenge while they negotiate constraining social structures" (xxi). Outside of the writing workshop, the writers with disabilities still had to negotiate significant "constraining social structures," whereas the organization's director, the university researcher, and those of us from the Community Writing Center did not. As Artz writes, "Rhetoric may enable the privileged to turn away, but for those that suffer the condition remains" (49). The writers' subtle and complex stories were a way for them to "obey and challenge," and do so on their own terms.

Further, the First Law of Ecology validates a focus on the individual. As Dobrin and Weisser state, "Our work can dramatically affect the individual lives of those with whom we come into contact (human and nonhuman) and can have valuable and significant effects in our communities in general—as long as we do not assume that these changes will occur overnight or that they will necessarily affect society as a whole" (101). For example, Stephen Parks's research into the Federation of Worker Writers and Community Publishers demonstrated that "voice operated on an individual and collective register," supporting both the person and the purpose (18). By following a rhetoric of respect for the individual's ability to make the best decisions, to seek self-determined changes, the CWC attempted to resist inadvertent exploitation and oppression that even the most progressive movements can impose on those they seek to empower.

WE KNOW WHAT YOU NEED TO KNOW

I'd like to take this discussion of a rhetoric of respect for the individual's wholeness and abilities and examine it a bit more in terms of how it affects relationships with activist/liberatory scholars and the people or communities with whom we wish to make change. A fundamental element of liberatory pedagogies has been Freire's concept of *conscientização*—critical consciousness—which is necessary for resistance of oppression. Acquiring critical consciousness requires that the oppressed "critically recognize [the causes]" of the systemic inequities to which they are subjected (*Pedagogy of the Oppressed* 47). Interpreting Freire for the US college classroom, Shor defines critical pedagogy (which fosters critical consciousness) as

> habits of thought, reading, writing, and speaking *which go beneath surface meaning*, first impressions, dominant myths, official pronouncements, traditional clichés, received wisdom, and mere opinions, *to understand the deep meaning, root causes, social context, ideology*, and personal consequences of any action, event, object, process, organization, experience, text, subject matter, policy, mass media, or discourse. (*Empowering Education* 129; emphasis added)

Similarly, Bruce Herzberg argues that service-learning projects that do not get at the social cause of inequity and make transparent American ideologies of meritocracy and the primacy of the individual result in perpetuation of the hegemonic structures of society that systemically disenfranchise certain groups and not others. He claims that students who engage in service need to come to the realization that the people they served at "Pine Street were not like them" in that they did not have the familial and social support, and access to education, that the students had (315). I agree that understanding causes and deep meanings of oppression and hegemonic structures can contribute significantly to disruption or resistance, but what I find most interesting in these frames is the implied necessity of an academic understanding for it to happen, which of course requires "someone else"—a liberatory teacher—to illuminate and unleash it.

Certainly, this is at least partly derived from the value that certain knowledges and critical ways of seeing the world has in challenging injustice. Yet framing academic intervention as essential to acts of resistance troubles me, particularly in the emerging discursive ecology of community literacy that, most often, asserts recognition of community partners' abilities and resources. Yet academic discourse continues to be seen as an essential requirement for change, for example, in Ackerman and Coogan's *The Public Work of Rhetoric: Citizen-Scholars and Civic Engagement*. In the foreword, Gerard A. Hauser writes that in order to be included in the decision-making processes in contemporary democracies, "as a society we require rhetors [academics] who can negotiate and translate technical problems to intelligent but less technically trained audiences" (xi–xii). Further, Carolyn R. Miller writes that the solution to "improving the state of our public life is an educational one. We need to teach citizens to listen, to find common ground, to seek good reasons for changing our minds" (31). In their arguments, both Hauser and Miller claim that "ordinary" people need scholars to alter their circumstances. Rarely, however, is it recognized that scholars cannot make progressive change on their own.

As I described earlier in the discussion about the Writing Partners program failure, the Community Writing Center learned early on that we could not determine methods of making change, nor could we make change by ourselves. Freire recognized this when he wrote that "many political and educational plans . . . have failed" because they were developed from a perspective available only to those with power (*Pedagogy of the Oppressed* 94). At the CWC, when we openly admitted our desire to make change and recognized the limitations of our resources, we could enter into collaborative relationships with other individuals and organizations seeking change. This is a subtle yet important factor in how the Community Writing Center was able to sustain itself and its community relationships over such a long period.

After our initial failures, the Community Writing Center pivoted from providing knowledge *to* partners into developing relationships based in a rhetoric of respect for multiple discursive ecologies, of which ours was an option, a choice, a possibility to contribute to collaborative change. Further, we embraced our literacy "sponsor" identity and acknowledged how the Community Writing Center "gain[ed] advantage" through working with individual writers and community organizations (Brandt, "Sponsors" 166). The Community Writing Center was not a selfless project, demarcated by sacrifice for the well-being of others. We worked hard, to be sure, but we benefited as well. The directors and writing assistants were paid to do intriguing and innovative work, build exciting relationships, and push against academic and literacy norms. The community college received recognition both locally and nationally for their investment in our experiment. Embracing our own self-interests in this work made space for the growth of a rhetoric of respect for others' purposes, interests, and priorities.

What this led to was a revision of our commitment to systemic or civic-focused change. Recognizing that the CWC was but one element of a relationship, with its own benefits to reap, meant that we also needed to respect the validity of what individuals and organizations chose to seek—or gain—from partnership with us. Prioritizing critical awareness of systemic injustice made the assumption that our partners lacked the knowledge that we needed to impart ("import") to them. Or else it alleged that our partners' ways of interpreting their circumstances were somehow inaccurate or inadequate. Doing so could only set the CWC up as yet another regulatory body that people would need to negotiate.

Returning to the relationship with the first DiverseCity Writing Series group, Dignity for Women (discussed in Chapter 2), I perceived the CWC's curriculum that explored self and community as necessary to the development of a critical consciousness that would lead to empowerment. Through writing prompts, participants would examine their systemic disenfranchisement and, as a result, increase their agency to challenge it. Obviously, this didn't happen. While a few wrote in response to the prompts, doing so did not increase their ability to fight oppression. At the end of the workshop, they were still poor, still sick, and still had family members stuck in jail.[12] However, the women did assert tangible agency against a particular systemic regulation: the curriculum and me—both symbols of a higher education institution they had been prevented from participating in.

Just like the writers in the folklore workshop, these women took over the purpose of the DWS group meetings. Most wrote what they wanted to write (or didn't come to the workshop meetings at all) yet still expected that their writing would be published in the group anthology—which it was. As I described earlier, this distressed me because I thought that I was necessary to an equation that might read "disenfranchised persons" + "activist academic" + "awareness-raising curriculum" = "potential empowerment." However, academic knowledge that can create an "awareness-raising curriculum" is just one way of interacting with the world, one that can be empowering to people who have the luxury of time and resources to devote to it. And sometimes acquiring such knowledge is not a priority for people living under unjust conditions. Grabill writes, "Programs and teachers cannot force critical consciousness after all, nor can they minimize personal and/or functional needs" (113). Of course, people outside of the academy, people subject to societal oppression, often take writing into their own hands to critique injustice (Parks 15). When activist teachers intervene in others' lives, though, we may expect that our goals will resonate since we likely derived much of our own sense of agency through developing critical awareness and intellectual agility. What becomes important, I believe, is how we respond to collaborations (how we pivot on the web) when our priorities and those of our partners don't necessarily match up. In such a situation, I believe the onus is on the activist teacher to step out of the equation she may have created and to adapt by remaining constantly vigilant of opportunities for partners' efforts to make self-determined change.

This is not particularly easy to do. Forgetting this critical point just for a moment played a role in how I interpreted the reading event for homeless youth at the CWC. Academic assumptions regarding the "prerequisites" of change can easily slip into the most well-intentioned projects. For example, David Coogan has collaborated often in community writing projects with a variety of partners. Coogan describes his role in working with teens on a community project as that of creating "middle spaces" (drawing from Susan Jarratt), which are "productive places to question the commonplaces or ideological statements" typically taken for granted ("Sophists" 159). After a middle space is created, Coogan says, he needs to "get out of the way" of the work that can take place within them ("Sophists" 172). However, in a prison writing project, Coogan leads several inmates in a county jail through an autobiography workshop, in which they were asked to "narrate their lives from the cause to the effect—to reason, morally, by making a story" ("David Coogan"). Of the nearly fifty men who began, only about twelve stayed with it to completion. Coogan writes that "guys who only wanted to tell street stories but wouldn't evaluate what they did and why, stuck it out a little longer but later drifted away." Rather than pivoting from a particular strand of the workshop's purpose and encouraging the possibilities of writing street stories, the workshop may have limited the writers' opportunities. To be fair, perhaps Coogan's workshop was subject to some of the policies that often regulate prison writing projects (Jacobi)—maybe jail administrators wanted only morality tales of intentions to reform. After facilitating a creative writing workshop for the Salt Lake County Jail, the Community Writing Center was invited to become part of their Life Skills program, in which the writing would require prisoners to morally examine their lives. Even so, within such ranges of tolerance, there is always flexibility; there is always space to establish a rhetoric of respect for the whole individual who enters into relationship with us as activist teachers, to honor spaces that we should not try to control. In an evaluation of the CWC's jail partnership, the sergeant responsible for the program said that the program demonstrated "ultimate creativity within a structure, but one that is interactive and open." Perhaps Coogan's street story writers could have been engaged with in a pivoted or shifted way, to build relationships outside of intended goals, and (maybe) create new spaces for change.

↬

As a program navigating the webs of higher education and community, the Community Writing Center had the capacity to bring a critical approach and intellectual resources to a partnership and to use those resources to resist the unjust circumstances within which some writers existed. At the same time, since one of our goals as a community partner was—at a minimum—to avoid or reduce institutional harm, we needed to be very careful not to impose our educational (institutional) assumptions on our partners—individuals or organizations. The CWC could have felt that certain curricula or collaborations might have led to a change in our partners' lives. However, if partners wanted to alter the meaning or parameters of our relationship, that option had to remain available to them without us terminating the relationship. Remaining invested in a collaboration by becoming flexible in our expectations was one way we demonstrated a rhetoric of respect for community members and partner organizations.

Although it could lead to uncomfortable uncertainty, this adaptive relationship appeared to be the most effective means for the Community Writing Center to contribute to change-making opportunities in the Salt Lake community. *Contribute* was the key term. As Parks argues, "Even when writing is our central area of expertise, we should not go it alone" (65).[13] As we entered into relationships, we carried three distinct yet inseparable assumptions with us. First, the Community Writing Center had resources to contribute to a potential partnership. Second, partnerships provided tangible benefits to the CWC in that they contributed to our ongoing arguments to the college to continue supporting the center. Third, and perhaps the most important, though we had resources and benefited from partnerships, we were equally ready to adapt the goals or processes of a particular relationship if that is what the partner desired, as long it did not counter CWC principles. As Paula Mathieu writes, "Too often faculty show up on [a] doorstep after they have an agenda, after defining a project, a class or a research idea. When academics enter a scene already carrying an agenda, they may fail to acknowledge and genuinely interact with people as individuals and instead view them only as means to an end" (63). The CWC acknowledged that a part of the value of partnerships was a "means to an end": sustaining the center so that other community members and organizations could use its resources. But at the same time, those means could bend and flex—and, admittedly, sometimes break apart into nonrelationship.

Even though the writing assistants, faculty directors, and I consciously brought these assumptions to the relationships we built with community members and organizations, ideologies of educational "empowerment" would sometimes break through and color how we interacted with certain writers or partnerships—in inadvertently disempowering ways. In a discussion about the Literacy Action Center group in the DiverseCity Writing Series, some of the writing assistants and I were debating the value of that group's writing, which, as I mentioned, tended to be very short nonfiction stories about writers or their families. Though we understood that many of the writers could produce only a paragraph or two, it seemed that after such a long time participating in the DWS program, the writers should be encouraged to move beyond personal expression toward analytical or critical engagement with the issues of their lives, or perhaps to enter into the imaginative world of fiction writing. Though we had done away with a curriculum that shaped what the writers would write about when the DWS became a noninterventional program, some of us were worried that the group's writers had settled into stasis, producing the same kind of writing year after year, and needed some kind of a push to continue their literacy development.

After listening to us debate options, intentions, and purposes, Melissa Helquist, who had been mentoring the group for two years, interrupted us in frustration: "You know, sometimes they just want to write stories. They want to forget for a moment about the fact that they can't read or write well enough to write a letter to a legislator, or to put together an argument. They know they're not 'literate enough,' but sometimes they just want to write stories like everyone else."[14] We looked at one another and realized that our discussion was categorizing the Literacy Action Center writers as "not quite whole" participants in the DiverseCity Writing Series, even though they were one of the first groups to join the program and were consistently more active than any other. We saw them as needing intervention, even though we didn't have the same concerns about the writers in the other DWS groups whose writing tended to be just as personal (not "analytical" or "critical") in both fiction and nonfiction narrative genres. Our concerns about the Literacy Action Center writing group dishonored the literacies they brought with them to the program and imposed an institutional value upon them. Jeff Grabill argues, "Those participating in the construction of community-based programs must be open to seeing and understanding the everyday literacies of their communities and local institutions. They are not only personally and communally meaningful, they are also a powerful currency of social interaction, status and well being" (104). The stories from the Literacy Action Center writers were as meaningful to them as the stories the other writers contributed to the published anthologies. Just like the other groups, the Literacy Action Center writers knew better than we did how they should spend their time and energy with writing.

Such misfires of good intentions can also happen in community writing projects when a partner (typically the institutional partner) falls into assumptions about what is "good for" those whom the project is intended to empower, and takes ownership over the writing produced within them, particularly when the writing becomes part of a tangible object such as a newsletter, anthology, zine, or other public document. At the Community Writing Center, we were reminded of this every six months when we compiled the *sine cera* publication. Because of our commitment to valuing writing regardless of its seeming complexity or "quality," each publication vowed to maintain the writing that a writer submitted in its original form, rather than editorially "improving" its quality. Each publication cycle, the writing assistant responsible for the anthology's production paid close attention to apparent "errors" and made limited changes, frequently consulting with other writing assistants when it wasn't clear that an error was simply a typo, or if concerned that a revision might alter the original meaning. (When we couldn't come to consensus, we would contact the writer, or the group's mentor if we didn't have access to the writer, for clarification.) Other projects show similar vigilance in prioritizing the writer/speaker's ownership of his words, as demonstrated by the work of the New City Community Press in publications like *Espejos y Ventanas* (*Mirrors and Windows*) and the publishing projects of the Neighborhood Story Project ("New City"). I'm sure we didn't always get it right, but we tried to be continually aware of how our interventions into the written words of our writers could become symbolically oppressive.

I was sitting at the front desk of the CWC one afternoon, covering for a writing assistant who needed to study for an exam. A woman came in quietly, nodded at me, and then began leafing through CWC publications that sat on the shelves near the front of the center. After a minute or so, I asked if I could help her with anything. She hesitantly replied that she had taken a writing class at the CWC and was really upset about what had happened during it. I asked her to sit down and tell me what happened.

She said that she had participated in a writing workshop for people with disabilities, that her writing had been published without her permission, and that changes had been made to it that she hadn't been told about. Recalling that an organization had used the CWC's classroom space for a writing workshop for people with mental disabilities a few months prior, I explained that hers wasn't a CWC workshop, but I still was concerned and asked her to tell me more (though I had trouble believing that this organization, with whom we had a long relationship, would do such a thing). She explained that on the first day, the participants were asked to sign a release form and were informed that they were to turn in their writing at the end of each workshop session. This sounded strange to me. Since I assumed the writers would be revisiting their work, I wondered if it was a way to keep their writing safe. The CWC had offered such writing storage for writers whose lives didn't allow them to keep track of their journals or electronic copies of their work. Still unsure of what had happened, I suggested that she write down her concerns and offered to help her share them with the organization's directors.

What appeared to have occurred was a set of seemingly innocuous mistakes on the organization's part, though they were mistakes that harmed the writer. First, the general release form didn't indicate where or how the writing would be published. In some community writing projects, organizers assume that participants want to make their writing public, though this is not necessarily the case. Mathieu describes a man in a writing group for homeless individuals: "Writing was integral and necessary to his life, but . . . being read by a wide public was unexpected and made him nervous" (37). The "open" release form placed the onus on the participant to track how her writing would be used. Second, the project's publication editor made several changes to her text. For example, the relative pronoun *that* was deleted from several sentences, unusual words (e.g., *wizened*) were made regular (*wise*), and adverbs were occasionally added for emphasis. While the changes may have been minor, they unnecessarily took away agency from this writer. I imagine that the editor actually wanted to "empower" the writer by making her writing "sound better." In making the text "whole," however, the editor positioned the writer as "not quite whole" and in need of revision. Unfortunately, these small changes caused the writer to lose faith in an organization that she had believed valued her and her abilities, rather than seeing her as something that needed to be fixed.[15]

~

When I interpreted the homeless youth reading event that began this chapter as not valuable, I spun a web that enclosed the event's worth inside its potential for change. But change can be had via many different intersections, and even if the CWC was a text-based space, its partners were more than that—they were organisms interacting in multiple and varied ways to create their own moments of change, moments that I had to remember to see. As Cushman argues, "If the subaltern cannot speak, it is only because the scholar cannot listen or hear" (*Struggle* 22). A glance at some data reveals that what we originally imagined would be empowering to community writers was not necessarily the case. While we prioritized opportunities to improve writing and to civically engage, writers tended to value most their experiences connecting with one another and writing stories. Although 85 percent of workshop participants reported that they signed up for a workshop to "improve [their] writing" and 89 percent of respondents strongly agreed that they had "gained new writing skills/abilities/ knowledge," the most frequently cited praise was that of human connection: "being able to share with others," "dialogue," "interaction between participants," and "please add more sessions so we can stay together." Perhaps making a space for homeless youth to come together in a semi-public arena with a respect for them as whole was in fact more valuable than anything they may or may not have written. Paula Mathieu's description of the "Not Your Mama's Bus Tour" would seem to support this interpretation. The tour brought together individuals living homeless in a writing and performance piece that played out over three weeks through the streets of Chicago. Mathieu writes that

> the project temporarily rewrote the strategic mandates affecting the writers' lives. . . . Twelve homeless writers/actors received pleasure, good experiences, and a job for six weeks. . . . At its best, perhaps this fleeting experience allowed the writers and producers a glimpse of a different life, where work is a meaningful act of creation. (45)

Although this kind of fleeting experience may not ascribe to academic or civic notions of change, perhaps creating spaces for people to temporarily rewrite their lives—according to their own interpretations of what is most necessary in a given moment—can be a powerful outcome of community writing projects. Such a construct does not necessarily work against projects that seek long-term or permanent change since individuals sometimes decide that collective action or systemic challenge is the appropriate path to take. The important point is that the academic partner needs to remain aware of its own self-interests while respecting the community partner's priorities.

BEFORE WE BECOME TOO CERTAIN OF OURSELVES . . .

Bertrand Russell writes, "The demand for certainty is one which is natural to man, but is nevertheless an intellectual vice" (26). Perhaps as a counter to that vice, we can look to Linda Flower's claim that "our certainties can be challenged when we recognize community partners as agents in their own right, rather than as the recipients of our service and empowerment" ("Intercultural" 184). Over time, drawing on our developing ease with uncertainty within the Community Writing Center, we came to embrace our uncertain relationships with partners and individuals, encountering them within a rhetoric of respect, taking on a responsive role rather than leadership, pursuing collaboration instead of empowerment.

Accordingly, I want to end this chapter with uncertainty. Though the Community Writing Center eventually came to an understanding of how we wanted to interact with community members and organizations, respecting them as whole persons capable of making the best decisions for themselves, the ecosystems surrounding the CWC and those we partnered with frequently called our role into question. The Community Writing Center's purpose was to make change possible by resisting educational and literacy systems of regulation. We were committed to a rhetoric of respect for our partners and their conceptions of what change might be. Even so, those partners existed within systems of social inequity, and while some were actively engaged in shared resistance, others were not. We engaged similarly with both in order to not impose academic notions of empowerment on them. When the partner organization, such as the Literacy Action Center, challenged hegemonic norms, our responsive and flexible approach seemed sound. When an organization was already empowered within society, however, I felt that the Community Writing Center found itself in a quandary: If our purpose was to resist oppressive power, what did we do when empowered agents sought our resources? If we worked with them, would the CWC reinforce inequality?

A look at the partnerships over the course of a single year, 2006–2007, illustrates this uncertainty. Many partnerships had a recognizable aura of change to them: college application essay workshops for high schools serving low-income students, collaborating with a youth government program to create documents to raise awareness of the problems stemming from "aging out" of foster care at eighteen years old, a series of writing workshops in collaboration with a theater production for African American women that celebrated the meaning of fancy Sunday-worn hats. But other partnerships felt as though they were merely perpetuating the status quo: an avant-garde poetry workshop and salon in collaboration with the city's professional ballet company; a daylong character development workshop for an annual romance writers' conference. Additionally, we entered into cross-promotional agreements and collaborations with a lifelong learning program that already catered to well-educated and well-financed communities. Was this the kind of work the SLCC Community Writing Center was supposed to be doing? At the same time, however, who were we to determine what was best for the community?

For me, this uncertainty increased significantly when we became a local partner with the national *This I Believe* (*TIB*) program sponsored by National Public Radio. The impetus for the partnership came from CWC staff members who enjoyed the program and wanted to make it more accessible to people who might not have had the confidence or the opportunity to submit their writing to the *TIB* website on their own. The *TIB* program was based on the 1950s radio show of the same name, hosted by acclaimed journalist Edward R. Murrow, which sought "to point to the common meeting grounds of beliefs, which is the essence of brotherhood and the floor of our civilization" ("This I Believe—History"). The original *This I Believe* program responded to fractures in 1950s US society, particularly those perpetuated by Senator Joseph McCarthy and his supporters. The contemporary program, which brought personal stories together in a type of public conversation, had gained traction with neoliberal, educated audiences who tended to affiliate with National Public Radio.

In three two-day workshops, CWC writing assistants collaborated with radio professionals from a local NPR-affiliated radio station to introduce participants to the history of the *This I Believe* program and provided instruction on crafting essays for the radio, time to share their writing, and tips for reading on the air. The workshops were filled to capacity—forty-five people participated, and an additional thirty people (mainly students in SLCC English

classes whose faculty included the assignments as part of their curriculum) submitted essays to the CWC. The local radio station staff
and CWC writing assistants selected ten essays to be read on the
program, which aired on a weekly basis for several months, giving
voice to those who otherwise may have gone unheard and providing significant positive public exposure for the CWC and the community college. It was a classic win-win situation, though I couldn't
help feeling uncomfortable—uncertain—about what its success
meant for the Community Writing Center.

The program likely made changes, however temporary or small,
in the lives of the people who participated in it. As I've shown, it
was not up to me or to the Community Writing Center to determine the worth of that change. That message had been reinforced
for me time and again at the center, and even outside of it by my
mother, who had always lived a life of socioeconomic stability. Even
though she held socioeconomic power, she kept her ideas to herself
"because the other person always sound[ed] so much smarter." As
the parent of a gay son, however, she was invited by a blogging
forum to contribute a post in response to the 2008 Proposition 8
in California that defined marriage as a union between one man
and one woman. Though she was afraid of "sounding stupid," she
wrote her post, "Why Do People Tell Other People They're Loved
but Not Equal?—This Essay Is Personal," and later called me to say
how great she felt that "people listened to [me] and didn't totally
disagree." Maybe it was a similar sort of valuable experience for
those who wrote "This I Believe" essays in the CWC workshops.

But there was something slightly different about the *TIB* program that made me feel uncertain, and not the "good" kind of uncertain that I was used to. I was conflicted about why this writing
project, rather than others, had such a great response. Was it because it didn't really challenge inequality and intolerance and simply created a forum for personal expression? Certainly other CWC
projects did that as well. Was it because the *TIB* project was an
already-established formula that the CWC imported into the community? I wasn't sure, but it drew attention to how the Community
Writing Center was adapting to its environment in order to survive.

The program's success highlighted the emerging institutionalization of the Community Writing Center, even though our intent was to resist the institutional power of higher education. I take up these questions in the final chapter, where I explore how institutionalization found its way back into the Community Writing Center (if indeed it had ever not been present) and into its relationships with the community.

5

Engaging Place: Acclimation and Disruption

January 2000: "Where do you want to be a year from now?"
"I want the CWC to be an actual place in the community."
January 2003: "Where do you want to be a year from now?"
"I want the CWC to formalize the structure of its programs."
January 2006: "Where do you want to be a year from now?"
"I want the CWC to be recognized as an institution."
January 2009: "Where do you want to be a year from now?"
"I want to go back to the beginning."

IN THE PREVIOUS TWO CHAPTERS, I USED ecocomposition theory to recognize change inside of (and in relation with) the SLCC Community Writing Center. First, ecocomposition helped to situate the CWC as a dynamic organism constituted by fluid groups of people who collaboratively developed a discursive ecology that deeply valued respect and welcomed uncertainty. Then I examined how the CWC, as an organism interacting with other organisms in the larger community and higher education ecosystems in Salt Lake City, built from our discursive ecology to recognize that change happens in ways we might not have anticipated or understood.

In this chapter, my inquiry into the Community Writing Center concludes with an examination of a central concern of ecocomposition: place. Out of several disciplines that inform ecocomposition, including cultural studies, ecofeminism, environmental rhetoric, and, of course, rhetoric and composition, ecocriticism was the one that raised the question, "In addition to race, class, and gender, should place become a new critical category?" (Glotfelty, in Dobrin and Weisser 25). Place is hardly apolitical, constructed as it is—physically and discursively—by political beings. Affirming its importance, Julie Drew argues that "the traditional and consequential submergence of the spatial within the temporal for critical social theory . . . effectively helps to veil institutional power within politicized spaces such as classrooms," when "politicized space is the location of hegemony" (59). Power—hegemonic or not—finds form inside of place.

Given the hybrid nature of the SLCC Community Writing Center, a higher education–based program that grew into a community-placed one, an examination of its relationship to place seems fundamental to recognizing change. Specifically, how did the CWC's original intentions to deroutinize educational and literacy hegemony respond to the pull of place, of sustainability, of institutionalization? In what ways did the CWC revise itself to acclimate to the requirements of survival? As Dobrin and Weisser argue, "Organisms must respond to changes in environment in order to survive; they must acclimate and they must maintain the ability to reverse those changes, to return to environments as they become more hospitable to habitation. Acclimation is the ability to change and change again." (76). For more than a decade, the CWC negotiated both physical and discursive place; it met ranges of tolerance that it pushed against, acclimated to, disrupted, and adjusted, while staying committed to recognizing and advocating for change opportunities within a rhetoric of respect.

A beginning pathway of inquiry into the CWC's relationship with place is through Paula Mathieu's *Tactics of Hope,* in which she uses Michel de Certeau's strategic/tactical binary to describe means of negotiating power in university–community partnerships:[1]

> [Certeau] describes *strategies* as calculated actions that emanate from and depend upon "proper" (as in propertied) spaces, like corporations, state agencies, and educational institutions, and relate to others via this proper space. . . . The goal of a strategy is to create a stable, spatial nexus that allows for the definition of practices and knowledge that minimize temporal uncertainty. (16)

The flip side of strategies is *tactics*, which Mathieu, again citing Certeau, describes as those actions that are available when one does not have a "proper" [space] from which to act (16). For example, Mathieu notes tactical responses made by a small advocacy organization to the unnecessary deaths of elderly low-income residents who could not afford to pay their heating or cooling bills. Because the advocacy group did not have a "proper," and therefore could not act strategically (such as mandating subsidized utilities), they could tactically respond by mailing holiday cards to lawmakers with provocative slogans such as "Jesus Christ Froze to Death" and stirring up responses in press releases that charged "How do you like your elders? Baked? Boiled? Or Fried?" (26). Although these tactics could not finally solve the problem, they could draw attention to the residents' deaths and need for intervention.

Mathieu explains how institutions (places)—including higher education—use policies, rules, time frames, deadlines, goals, outcomes, and formal assessments to regulate relationships. It is these strategies that Flower cautioned me against (see Chapter 4): determining success through institutional measurements. An aspect of regulating relationships, Mathieu highlights, is the way higher education often situates the community as outside the boundaries of institutionalized space through strategy that "postulate[s] a *place* that can be delimited as its own and serve as a base from which relations with an *exteriority* . . . can be managed" (Certeau 36). The trouble with identifying higher education–community partnerships as community "outreach" stems from this "place/exteriority" juxtaposition. Though much of this work is revising itself as "engagement" in response to such exteriorizing metaphors, in practice strategy still plays a significant role in partnership work.

A complementary entry point for place-based inquiry is through Foucault, as John Caputo and Mark Yount illustrate in *Foucault and the Critique of Institutions*: "Situat[ing] the institution within the thin but all-entangling web of power relations[,] . . . institutions are the means that power uses, and not the other way around" (4). As such, institutions and their places are tools through which power can welcome difference, while at the same time determine that which is "normal" and that which must be changed or regulated. Caputo and Yount write, "The norm has tolerances for a vast range of individuals, a duction[2] ample enough to promote diversity even as it constrains all deviations by its standard measure" (6). Institutions provide a discursive range of tolerance for organisms that exist within them, wish to enter them, or strive to resist them. Ultimately, however, power requires acclimation, which "can be likened to Cooper's web, in which the writer must move into the web in order to be heard, and frequently is subsumed by the web and the writer's disturbances of the web absorbed and consumed" (Dobrin and Weisser 106). For power to maintain itself, difference must be tolerated even as difference is constrained and regulated through strategy and institution (through *place*).

Certeau argued that tactics are tools of the place-less. Accordingly, the first Community Writing Center partnership—before the CWC was a "place"—was a tactical engagement. This partnership attempted to deroutinize practices typical of higher education norms. One tactic was to hold the Dignity for Women Diverse-City Writing Series project in their organization's offices and local cafés—not on college property. When I think back to that first relationship, I remember a cold evening in November 2000, pulling my car into a parking stall in front of Cup of Joe's café west of downtown for the first celebration of a DiverseCity Writing Series publication. I carried in a box of the photocopied and saddle-stapled zine, *Wisdom in Words,* that the writers in the Dignity for Women group had created. I returned to my car, lugged a speaker and microphone out of the trunk, and took them into the warmth of the building. As I set up the equipment next to the coffee roasting barrel, the writers trickled in, a few with friends or family, the rest alone. We dragged metal tables and chairs across the cement floor to create an audience space as the espresso machine screeched in the background. Café patrons chatted with one another, glancing over to see what we were doing, and then going back to their own business.

When it seemed that everyone had arrived, I welcomed the twenty or so people. A few called out "Talk louder!" so I turned up the speaker and unleashed a feedback squeal that made the rest of the café look over in annoyance. After apologizing, I invited Beth to read. She stepped up to the mic and read her essay, "Dignity for Women." In turns, five more women shared writing that emerged either directly or tangentially from our writing workshop. After the final reader, we opened up the floor to questions. A few audience members made supportive comments, everyone applauded, and we snapped several group pictures. As we went our separate ways, I thanked the café's barista, hauled the equipment back to my car, and drove away, feeling as though we had accomplished something. We had stepped off the sticky web of higher education by ceding to the women the authority over—and meaning of—the partnership. Low-income women learned on their own terms, in their own time frames, for free.

This project was a small, and momentary disruption to the order of higher education, one well tolerated by institutional norms. Many higher education–community partnerships find similarities with the CWC's Dignity for Women partnership—temporary programs tactically facilitated in off-campus locations. In the years since that workshop, however, a distinguishing feature of the SLCC Community Writing Center became its place-ness, its propertied space—or, in other words, its institutional status, both in the community and in the college.

Even though the CWC was developed in response to what we considered limiting forces of certain institutions, to create what Parks refers to as "oppositional moments" (49), it was always intended to be a place. Though they emerged separately, both Stephen Ruffus's and Susan Miller's original concepts for such a center assumed a physical space external to academic property. We believed a writing center sited in the community could create an alternative to hegemonic structures that determined what (and whose) literacies were valid and the means by which people could acquire new literacies. As is required to establish place, the CWC worked toward institutionally recognized symbols of stability; in other words, we worked strategically. When a small group of faculty and community members came together in 1999 to write a mission statement and founding assumptions, years of ideas and messy thoughts coalesced into a solid purpose. When the CWC opened in the Artspace Bridge Projects in 2001, it transformed from a purpose and activities into a physical space (with an address and phone number) that people could enter into, where they could talk, collaborate, create, and explore. In this place, the Community Writing Center was a space of experimentation, where failure and success were valued equally. When the CWC moved to Library Square, it had to become more strategic, to evolve new organizational structures, policies, and multilayered partnerships with government institutions and community agencies. At Library Square, it was time to "grow up" (i.e., show institutional signs of professionalism) since the center had become a very public face—perhaps ambassadorial—of the community college.

Eight years after the Dignity for Women public reading event, I stood at another microphone, this one set up for us, to welcome a sold-out audience to the first annual fundraiser for the SLCC Community Writing Center.[3] Held at the SLC Arts Council's "Art Barn" gallery, the evening's readers were eight elementary school children who had won the CWC's haiku writing contest. After the children finished reading their seventeen-syllable poems, SLCC President Cynthia Bioteau spoke admiringly of the CWC and articulated its centrality to the college's mission. During the rest of the evening, donors filled their stomachs with food donated from local restaurants and placed silent bids on dozens of framed haiku poems contributed by local and national authors and public figures such as Julia Alvarez and Craig Childs, former Utah Governor Jon Huntsman, and Salt Lake Mayor Ralph Becker. Packaged with donated items such as Utah Jazz basketball tickets, walking history tours of downtown Salt Lake, and luxury spa treatments, the bids rose higher and higher.

At the end of the evening, the auction winners paid for their prized possessions, and we loaded leftover food, drinks, brochures, anthologies, flowers, plates, and cutlery into our cars. The college president, city mayors, state governors, and government programs had contributed their time, energy, and resources to a program that had begun as a decidedly anti-institutional experiment. What emerged from resistance to socioeconomic inequities had acclimated to them, capitalizing on the disposable income of people who wished to contribute to a good cause. As I drove away, I realized that the CWC had become, in Certeau's words, "a subject of will and power" (xix).

PLACE MATTERS

About the same time as the fundraiser, the college was starting to respond to the impact of the 2008 national recession. Although Utah was not hit as hard as some other states, the Utah System of Higher Education sustained deep cuts, translating into double-digit budget reductions at SLCC. Cuts across all areas of the college started in the fall of 2008, yet by the winter holidays, the CWC was still untouched. That would change in late January 2009, when my dean delivered the news that budget cuts meant the CWC was going to take some personnel reductions and, more important, was to relocate from Library Square onto an SLCC campus located across the street in a leased four-story office building.

Concerns about place are common to student writing centers; physical and institutional location is an ongoing issue of debate. Haviland, Fye, and Colby describe a politics of place that "creates visibility or invisibility, access to resources, and associations that define the meanings, uses, and users of designated spaces" (85). The SLCC Community Writing Center's place on Library Square—and previously at the Artspace Bridge Projects—engaged directly with accessibility and meaning, stretching the limitations of who could be considered a writer—and when they could write. Its street-level placement, with a door opening to the outside, meant that CWC staff—not the college or the library—could determine its hours of operation. It could be open early or late, on Sundays and holidays, to respond to community requests. Additionally, as I discussed earlier, the off-campus location made it more possible to disrupt the roles and identities assigned to bodies in educational institutions (e.g., student, teacher, administrator, staff). One particular disruption was heard nearly every day when someone entered the CWC only to ask hesitantly, "Do I need to be a student to come in here?" This uncertainty was always met with a resounding "No!" from around the center.

This "No!" sounded again throughout the SLCC Community Writing Center when we were told the center was moving to a college campus. To administrators concerned with the black and white of budgets, saving a few thousand dollars a year on rent superseded the importance of location. They were also aware that the CWC's dynamic presence in the community raised the possibility that such a move would invigorate the new downtown SLCC property.

Those of us at the CWC believed the move would impact real and perceived access to the CWC. The mere fact that the CWC would lose its all-important front door was significant to us, not to mention the additional barriers faced by nonstudents on a college campus. Though the leased building also housed a couple of nonprofit organizations and some legal offices, a huge "Salt Lake Community College" sign outside plainly marked the space as a place of higher education. To access the CWC, nonstudents would need to be willing to step onto the campus where they may well not feel they belonged, and even before that, they would have to have the confidence to argue with parking attendants about why they should be able to use student parking stalls. Some CWC writers possessed such self-authority, though not nearly enough of them.

While we deeply appreciated that SLCC administrators wanted to maintain the CWC in some form rather than shut it down altogether as had been suggested five years earlier, we did not accept the argument that we should "be grateful for any kindness," an expectation familiar to student writing centers and community literacy workers whose programs do not generate full-time-equivalent student resources and therefore should be thankful for *any* space, for *any* budget. We were reminded of this often—"In this budget crisis, you should consider yourselves lucky"—and for a moment, I wondered whether our insistence on staying put was a selfish response. To us, however, the move threatened the CWC's entire identity. Ultimately, to a person, the staff agreed that location was of the utmost importance. In our counterproposal to administrators, Andrea Malouf wrote:

The Importance of Place

People relate differently to a public space (the Plaza, owned by the City of Salt Lake, and thus the community) and to an institutional space (a college campus, including an urban one). **People feel they belong to—and in fact own—public spaces**; on the other hand, people encounter real and/or perceived barriers when they enter institutional spaces. While the SLCC Library Square campus is just across the street from the Plaza, and is eager for community interaction, as a college campus, it is not a public space. This affects the mental access, the feeling of "do I belong?," that people will have to the Community Writing Center should it be moved there. Because of that, **access to educational opportunity** is at stake . . . . At the SLCC Strategic Planning Retreat in the fall[,] [c]ommunity leaders stated loudly and clearly that they wished to partner with the college, but that partnerships needed to be collaborative and "not only on the College's terms." **The CWC is a fully-developed instance of the College meeting the community on their terms, rather than asking them to cross perceived boundaries of institutional difference.**

Along with this argument, we proposed a plan to pay for the CWC's rent through workshop fees and included two-dozen letters and emails of support from community representatives and activist scholars from across the country. Three weeks of intense negotiations up the chain of command, punctuated mostly by insistence that the decision was already made, eventually came to SLCC President Cynthia Bioteau. During a tense meeting[4] with President Bioteau, two members of the CWC Community Advisory Committee, Dean John McCormick, and the director of the City Library, we learned that Bioteau had been persuaded by our arguments. She allowed the CWC to remain in place.

Through this decision, Salt Lake Community College maintained an anomalous learning place[5] that people entered while sometimes noticing the "Salt Lake Community College" logo above the door and sometimes not. Once inside, they may have learned that the CWC was part of the community college, or they may not have. Perhaps they pivoted a little bit in their relationships with writing and education; maybe they turned in their relationship with SLCC. People who might never have imagined themselves in a community college for reasons of perceived inferiority (or superiority)[6] found themselves already in one—albeit one that didn't neatly fit their expectations; it pushed the norm's range of tolerance.

A FALSE BINARY

The Community Writing Center's commitment to place was one strategy in its drive toward stability and, correspondingly, institutionalization. In the years leading up to the budget crisis, tension developed between its acclimation to institutionalized status and the center's original purpose. At times I found myself asking whether the CWC strayed too far from our principles and intentions in order to sustain it, or perhaps I was foolishly hanging on to the ideals set forth in conversations with Ruffus and Miller, a challenge that many founders face. Two specific instances illustrate the difficulties of this transition.

About two years after the CWC moved to Library Square, we sponsored the "This I Believe" essay project discussed at the end of the previous chapter. This was a very successful project that brought significant exposure to the CWC and provided a forum for dozens of community members to express themselves publicly. SLCC administrators who heard the essays repeatedly played on the radio called to share their praise. The Institutional Marketing department calculated the public relations value of this project to the college to be more than $7,000. Writers responded with high praise in workshop evaluations, and the radio station with which we collaborated was eager to repeat the partnership. Even so, I could not shake the discomfort that this project was not what the CWC was supposed to be doing. My concern was twofold. First, National Public Radio (NPR), which sponsored the *This I Believe* program,[7] is an important resource to many people, though without a doubt its listeners are more educated, have more money, and are more politically engaged than the average person living in the

United States.[8] Ruffus, Miller, and I did not have an NPR audience in mind when we imagined whom the CWC might support. The *TIB* project participants might not have been NPR audience members—a demographic we did not measure for—but even so, the middle-class discourse that the *TIB* project promoted hinted at hegemonic regulation of difference. The writing explored aspects of love, illness, friendship, animals, faith, childhood, and respect— safe expressions of self and belief, not rebukes of a McCarthy-dominated national discourse as was the original *This I Believe* series.

As I also mentioned in the previous chapter, I felt that the Community Writing Center should not determine the kind of writing acts people engaged in, but I could not help but compare the reception of the *This I Believe* project to the Dignity for Women partnership. In that project, the Dignity for Women writers wrote about poverty, police brutality, stolen children, nuclear reactors, and suicide attempts—and did so on their own terms, not within the format I had intended for them. Their writing was sporadic, disjointed, and self-focused, not crafted into orderly three-minute radio essays. I wondered whether the Dignity for Women's voices would have received so much praise if aired over public radio stations with SLCC's name attached to them (or whether a radio station would have aired them at all).

Certeau writes that "lacking its own place . . . a tactic is determined by the absence of power just as a strategy is determined by the postulation of power" (37). Subsequently, Mathieu claims that an institutional (place-based) lens colors how universities envision community partnerships: "Most of the means for designing, launching and evaluating street initiatives originate within universities and . . . rely on institutional logics or student outcomes for evaluating teaching or research" (15). Because the outcomes of tactics are "temporary and fleeting[,] . . . not easily measurable[,] . . . their overall effects are not always clear," and higher education often fails to recognize their value (33).

It was precisely this distinction I was concerned about. The Dignity for Women partnership was tactical, temporary, and place-less. The *This I Believe* program was institutional; it was an already codified process of self-expression that we imported into the space of the Community Writing Center, where we transferred a selection of those expressions (judged to be "the most representative") into a mainstream radio space. This was quite different from the Diverse-City Writing Series program, of which the Dignity for Women group was the pilot project, in which all writers wrote what they wished, in whatever form, and were all published together without judgment of quality. Perhaps the radio station and college administrators would have valued the Dignity for Women's writing just as much, though it would have surprised me. Regardless, the praise heaped on the CWC for the *This I Believe* project was unlike any we had seen before. While I certainly appreciated it, and was thankful for the way it boosted both the community's and the college's confidence in the CWC, its smooth success unnerved me.

A year and a half later, during the budget crisis, the Community Writing Center entered into a formal agreement with our landlord, the City Library, to exchange services for partial rent reduction. The library's willingness to do so played an important role in our negotiations with college administrators, and it institutionally benefited the library as well. Though the CWC had been partnering with the library in an ad hoc manner for many years, library administration wanted more oversight of, and decision-making power over, these collaborations. Together we agreed on a package of projects, including one to replicate a mentoring program run by the New York nonprofit Girls Write Now, in which teenage girls are paired in mentoring relationships with women who use writing in their professional lives.[9] Library administrators asked us to head up development of this project (which we named Salt Lake Girls Write) in collaboration with three library staff members.

On the surface, the Salt Lake Girls Write (SLGW) program seemed to align quite well with the principles of the Community Writing Center. The shape of the mentoring relationships fit nicely within our Writing Coaching pedagogies—the interactions focused on writing development rather than writing quality, and the overall goal was to provide alternative learning opportunities for teenage girls in vulnerable socioeconomic circumstances. In proposal documents, we attempted to infuse a rhetoric of respect into the program by suggesting that rather than a "uni-directional mentoring program . . . where the mentors have the knowledge and the mentees receive it . . . the CWC would like to design a program that taps into the resources of both the mentor and the mentee, and design outcomes in which both give and both gain."[10] As the SLGW program took shape, however, a meaningful difference between its development and the typical evolution of CWC programs began to emerge.

Along with library staff, we made decisions about the SLGW program without talking to individuals or organizations (e.g., teachers or schools) directly involved in the lives of the girls we imagined would participate. Our group had agreed that was the job of the library staff, and we left it to them, even though it soon became obvious that they were having little success. Contrary to the CWC's common practice (yet strikingly similar to the *This I Believe* project), we imported a program and modified it for our local environment based on groundless assumptions. We ignored our relationships with the larger community and worked within a client (institutional) relationship with the library, establishing the CWC as the provider of specific elements of a program, not as a collaborator with the community. As a consequence, we made thoughtless mistakes, such as distributing applications and parent/guardian permission forms only in English when a simple conversation with teachers would have made it obvious that Spanish-language documents were essential.

With the financial pressure to make the program a success for our landlord-client, we disregarded our rhetoric of respect as we promoted the program to potential mentors. Assuming that middle-class, educated women would be more motivated to volunteer if they were helping "the less fortunate," we created calls for mentors that read, "The Salt Lake City Public Library and the SLCC Community Writing Center are seeking volunteer mentors for **at-risk** young women (ages 16–17) in a new community writing program to begin September 2010" (emphasis added). I can't remember when, or if, we had ever used the term *at-risk* beyond the original CWC proposal documents, but certainly not after we had moved physically into the community. Still, I made the decision to do so, to frame certain high school girls as "not quite whole." When Rachel Meads angrily called me out on it, I knew she was right but bluntly responded, "Sometimes you've gotta play the game by those rules," and turned away, knowing that, at that moment, the CWC had pivoted (or acclimated) to a different relationship with the community, and myself to being a different kind of director.[11] The pressures of institutionalization were slowly eroding the pleasures of uncertainty that had for so long formed the CWC's discursive ecology.[12]

Mathieu argues, "The more we rely on strategic models, which seek stability instead of specificity, the more marginalized and disregarded will be the everyday voices and opinions of those in the streets and neighborhoods we seek to serve" (xiv). With the center's "place" on the line, we defaulted to a strategic model that threatened to disregard the voices of those we purported to be in partnership with. Yes, the CWC was successful, was becoming more and more stable and a part of the fabric of the community, but at what price? As I entered my final year at the Community Writing Center, my primary goal was to shore up its standing in the community and in the college, and to reinforce its internal infrastructure so that it could continue its work into the future. Each of these efforts—and those that had come in the previous years—involved a further level of institutionalization, and I worried that the strategic logics necessary to its process would prevent the CWC from resisting regulatory systems as we had set out to do. As Mathieu writes, strategies tend to maintain, rather than change, power relationships, so "thinking strategically [about community partnerships], then, *is not an option*, because the dynamic spaces where we work should not be considered strategic extensions of academic institutions" (17; emphasis added). Similar to Ellen Cushman's critique of liberatory terms of change, Mathieu argues for a redefinition of "what we consider a 'success story'" (20), one that would "consider more local tactical options as well" (96).

On reflection, I imagine that Mathieu did not mean to draw the line between strategies and tactics so starkly,[13] though my doing so draws attention to how easy it is to oversimplify complex ways of relating—which, I believe, was at the base of my concern: if the center institutionalized, it would become unavoidably oppressive in our relationships. However, relationships are much messier than that. In our drive for sustainability, the CWC engaged in strategic relationships that contradicted our original intentions, some more than others. At the same time, even while acting strategically, the CWC continually cycled through tactical responses—taking the "form not of long-term problem amelioration but limited-term projects" (Mathieu xix). Tactics shake the web of institutional regulation but do not break the strands. And while strategy may be the means to maintain the system, it is not limited to doing so; instead, strategy can build new strands on the web to disrupt inequities. These strands may not remake the web, but they create new intersections and possibilities for change. Through strategy the norm's range of tolerance can be pushed further, and for longer, when used in concert with tactical engagement. The simultaneous engagement with tactic and strategy was how the CWC built new strands and gave away institutional power.

Two primary features of tactics are their temporal nature and uncertain outcomes. Although the CWC was a place, most (if not all) of its programs were place-less, crafted to adapt to the particular partners, contexts, and audiences with which we were working. For example, one of the CWC's first partnerships (see Chapter 3) was with a drug detox center that used writing as a part of their recovery program. The staff requested brief and repeatable workshops (to accommodate short attention spans) to address the "writer's block" that constricted their clients' ability to complete their programs. Though nearly 100 people participated in these workshops in one year, privacy policy prevented us from learning whether the workshops had an effect on recovery completion. In another partnership, this one lasting for three years, the CWC collaborated with an antipoverty nonprofit to offer a "Writing to Public Officials" workshop as a part of their annual Citizen Advocacy Day at the state legislature. Approximately 200 people took part in these workshops, and certainly some of them did write to their legislators and other public officials. Still, systemic and long-term issues of poverty continued unabated. On a similar note, after we had thoroughly established our place at Library Square, we partnered with Salt Lake City in a science and art event that promoted environmental quality. The CWC sponsored a project for children to write postcards to the SLC mayor and the Utah governor about the importance of clean air and water. More than 100 postcards were hand-delivered to their offices and the CWC received friendly notes of recognition in return. But no environmental policy revision was implemented by the city or the state.

Certeau aligns tactics with the art of the sophistic (38) and the kairotic use of the appropriate moment. Accordingly, Mathieu claims that tactics seek "not stability but clever uses of time" and available resources (17). Such actions may or may not result in the outcomes that one intends:

> Tactical projects . . . operate in the realm of the indirect and the possible. . . . Someone may decide to kick heroin. A reader may change how he or she feels about the homeless man asleep on the corner. Someone may finally learn word processing or improve academic literacy skills. Certain problems may disappear or decrease. . . . But then again, they might not. (xix)

None of the above-mentioned partnerships resulted in systemic change, yet they capitalized on the resources of the moment (e.g., people, knowledges, motivations, abilities) within a specific time and space (e.g., events, organizations, pressing issues) to temporarily disrupt or deroutinize the power that institutions hold over people.

The tactical relationships between the CWC and the community were echoed in the relationship between the CWC and Salt Lake Community College. Instead of institutionally regulating its participants (CWC writers were not required—or even asked—to register as students of the college), the college may have recognized the center as a space of possibility rather than strategic outcome. In early proposal documents, we claimed that the CWC would "create . . . a direct link to the higher education possibilities and to the programs offered at Salt Lake Community College."[14] In other words, we believed that administrators would support the CWC if it generated a more diverse student body for the college.[15] That link was never documented, which didn't appear to be a problem for SLCC administrators, who already saw the CWC fulfilling the community college's mission. President Bioteau commented,

> It's lovely that perhaps a person may come to the Community Writing Center and say, "I've done this, maybe I should take a course at the college," and probably that happens, but [the CWC is] far deeper in its rooting in the importance of the community college than that direct correlation of "I came to the community writing center, I learned another component of my writing ability and now I'm taking a course."

Perhaps for Bioteau, the CWC was a means of engaging tactically inside of higher education's regulatory norms, and as Mathieu writes, with tactics, things may happen; then again, they may not.

Even as the Community Writing Center was tactically disrupting norms, it used strategy to do so as well. The CWC employed the politics of its place to press toward providing alternative literacy education within a rhetoric of respect. The strategic fight to maintain the center's space on Library Square was one instance of this work; remaining in that location guaranteed access for community writers that they would not otherwise have had. Acting strategically also allowed us to enter into formal agreements with the City Library that bolstered the center's stability—even though these agreements sometimes were problematic—and led to more partnerships between the CWC and multiple library branches on a wide range of projects. Overall, the specific location—and institutional relationships—the CWC fought for led to opportunities to make significant changes in the literacy landscape of Salt Lake City, one of which I describe here.

The Utah Arts Festival is an annual event that draws 80,000 people to the Salt Lake City and County Building park space and Library Square each summer for four days of art, music, dance, food, and partying. When the Community Writing Center moved to Library Square in January 2006, we knew that in six months, tens of thousands of people would be just outside our front doors. On the Saturday afternoon (typically the biggest day) of that year's festival, we strung a huge banner across the top of our front doors announcing a "mini-workshop-a-thon": free forty-five-minute writing workshops in creative journaling, graphic novels, and slam poetry. We taped poster-size paper to the windows and invited the community to write open letters, memos, poems, and stories on any topic of their choice. Without asking permission of the Utah Arts Festival (UAF), we tactically capitalized on their temporary presence to increase community awareness of the CWC.

Immediately after the 2006 festival, I contacted the UAF director to see if we might partner in an official capacity, offering to provide workshops, stage readings in the CWC, or supply local writers from the CWC's DiverseCity Writing Series to their literary performances. She passed me on to the festival's literary arts coordinator, who hadn't heard of the CWC but was interested in our air-conditioning to escape the sometimes 100°F heat; she suggested staging some reading and multimedia performances inside the center during the 2007 festival. Though not ideal, this was an opportunity to showcase the CWC's space for very little effort. It didn't quite work out as planned, of course, and misunderstandings resulted in situations legally worrisome, physically dangerous, and ethically questionable for the CWC and its staff. Open flames during a performance risked burning the CWC down; belligerent artists and insufficient security for the large and inebriated crowds threatened the safety of the writing assistants. Some of the performers read incendiary works that could have been interpreted as racist and abusive, compromising both the CWC's and the college's reputation in the community and potentially violating institutional hate speech policies.

At the end of the 2007 festival, we decided that the only way to work with the UAF was strategically. We wrote a proposal that would, in our eyes, enhance the festival's literary programming and also allow us to retain control over the CWC's environment and offerings. At the same time, our proposal sought to redefine who was a "literary artist" in the community, which had been limited to a recycled lineup of local poets and writers who had published or had received literary recognition. Agreeing with the CWC's proposal, the Utah Arts Festival added a participatory community-based approach to their performer-centric literary arts norm. The following year, and each after that, kids and adults stopped into the CWC to write flash fiction and rock poetry, advocacy letters, and fairy tales. Thousands of festivalgoers contributed to massive community writing projects, covering the windows and walls of the center with mini-autobiographies written on sticky notes or racing one-minute sand timers to compose a moment's worth of poetry. The DiverseCity Writing Series writers shared their writing with curious crowds and distributed their publications to audiences who didn't know that community members could write and be published just as the heralded literary artists were.

Though location could be used to make change, the CWC's location on Library Square also contributed to one of the most significant challenges I faced while I was there: its co-optation by middle-class, educated community members and organizations. As I mentioned, when the City Library offered a space for the center on Library Square, Melissa Helquist and I were slightly concerned about how the location would affect access for people without stable housing, given that this population mostly resided in the shelter across the street from the Artspace Bridge Projects or in the parks just nearby. Still, we reasoned that Library Square and the City Library were as welcoming an environment as possible to people in these life circumstances—the entire block was passionately defined by the community as a public space and library administrators were committed to it as such. As it turned out, most people who used the CWC while it was located at the Artspace Bridge Projects continued to do so after our move, but we hadn't foreseen (perhaps ignorantly) how the increased public exposure would dramatically alter the demographics of people who used the center—and as a result, the programming we offered there.

While the ethnicity of writers at the CWC remained fairly stable after our move, with nearly a third being writers of color, income and education levels shifted significantly. During its first two years, while at the Artspace Bridge Projects, three out of every four writers had annual household incomes below federal poverty levels, likely because people living at the shelter often stopped in to use one of our five computers (which constituted one of the few public Internet access points in Salt Lake at that time). Most came in to check their email; some stayed to work on writing or enjoy some conversation. When the City Library opened in 2003, many of these people opted for the library's new computer lab (where they could get away from our constant monitoring of their computer activities to be sure they were doing "writing-related work"), and the percentage of low-income writers dropped over the next two years to 48 percent. Many stayed, however, becoming part of the CWC's collection of relationships: writing, volunteering, and participating in groups and workshops. However, this income group's participation dropped further when the CWC moved to Library Square in 2006. In just a year and a half, the percentage of low-income writers slumped to 31.5 percent. It wasn't necessarily that lower-income writers had stopped participating; rather, higher-income groups discovered the center once it was located in the middle-class space of Library Square. When the center was across from the homeless shelter, only 18 percent of writers made more than $50,000 a year; in just two years at the library, nearly 32 percent of newly registered writers placed themselves in that income bracket.

Educationally, the trajectories were similar. When we started out, nearly 62 percent of writers had their GED or a high school diploma, 32.5 percent had associate or bachelor's degrees, and 2.8 percent had master's degrees or PhDs. Stephen Ruffus and I had intended that the CWC's main audience would be people considered literate by societal standards but who felt ill-equipped to enter new literacy situations. Therefore, we aimed for a balance between high school and college graduates. By our third year, this balance seemed to be established, with a percentage of college degree–holders (associate and bachelor's) nearly equal to that of those with high school education (and people who had not completed a high school degree).[16] However, the move to Library Square caused a significant jump in writers with college or advanced degrees. Within a year, nearly 60 percent of writers had college degrees and another 14 percent had advanced degrees, whereas just 23.7 percent had only their high school diplomas.

In our move to Library Square, Helquist and I realized that "becoming visible meant becoming an object of scrutiny and control," and that people in positions outside of those "most intimately connected" to the CWC's "founding objectives" had a much larger stake in it now (Parks 62). In response, we began drafting the Foundational Principles; we wanted to codify that the center's values were based on education, community, and collaboration. This work took us nearly a year and included important statements such as "The CWC is a place of learning," "Students should always be a part of the CWC staff," "CWC programs must be available to everyone," and "The CWC actively seeks out partnerships with communities and individuals who have been traditionally underserved by higher education." At the same time, this document reflected how we sought to build relationships and included particular statements that placed the ownership of CWC programming with the community: "CWC collaborations should always be guided by our partner in learning and focused on developing new writing knowledge," and "CWC programming is responsive to community requests and inquiries; the CWC does not determine what the community's writing needs and desires are."

My commitment to these latter priorities likely prevented me from confronting how the Community Writing Center seemed to be morphing into a place for educated, well-off community members. While it did cause stress within the CWC staff—we often debated the appropriateness or relevance of particular partnerships to the CWC's mission—we kept going back to the mantra that the CWC did not decide what the community needed. Additionally, a dramatic increase in community requests for partnership, a rapidly growing demand for writing coaching, and formalized institutional partnerships kept us hopping from one moment to the next. There was little time for reflection on what was happening to the center.

Even though a legitimate concern of moving higher education

properties into the community (e.g., satellite campuses, centers) is that higher education may assert power inappropriately over that community, at the Community Writing Center it appeared the opposite was happening: in our efforts to sustain the center, both strategically (with public and institutional support) and tactically (by sticking to our principles of collaboration), the CWC was acclimating to serving an economically and educationally privileged community. In doing so, we entered into projects and partnerships that did indeed maintain systemic power relationships—or at the very least, ignored them. The avante-garde poetry workshop and ballet performance were fun but not exactly "disruptive," nor was the CWC's participation in the National Novel Writing Month (NaNoWriMo), nor the increasingly playful writing workshops we offered, including spooky stories for Halloween or love letters for Valentine's Day. Additionally, overwhelmed by the influx of requests and activity, we stopped actively seeking out partnerships with underserved community members and organizations. The quantitative growth of the Community Writing Center—more writers, more workshops, more partnerships, more writing groups, more publications—coupled with the validation that the "community" was taking more ownership of the center, masked the fact that the CWC was moving away from its purpose to deroutinize hegemonic literacy education.

In both of the Community Writing Center's locations, the open-access environment created space for community members to assert ownership over it. Its place-ness made it possible to give the college's institutional power away, at least temporarily. At the Artspace Bridge Projects, individuals asserted their intentions to do what they wanted in the center's space: surf the Internet for soft-porn sites (until we told them not to), use the tables as their personal office spaces (because they had none), while away the day reading and sleeping in the classroom (again, because they had no place of their own). However, these personal assertions were not sustainable in an environment intended for literacy education activities and that had the authority of an educational institution behind it. Though the CWC writing assistants and I had many discussions about just what the center's space in the Artspace Bridge Projects could be used for, our typical response to such "transgressions" was to introduce another policy regulating behavior: no Internet surfing, no sleeping, no spreading out stuff across multiple tables. At the Library Square location, however, assertions of community ownership were within the range of tolerance for what could be considered "literacy education"—writing workshops and reading events. As such, community requests could be located within the center's mission. The improved stability the CWC gained from these projects added to their apparent value. Just like the partnership with the Utah Arts Festival, building strategic relationships with individuals and institutions of privilege was important to the sustainability of the center. But with the exception of the UAF partnership, we weren't using our new status and stability regularly in determined efforts to disrupt or make change.

In some ways, the budget crisis and threat to move the Community Writing Center to a college campus couldn't have come at a better time because it served as a wake-up call for us to define what the CWC was. Even though college administration heaped praise on the *This I Believe* project, it was not this kind of work through which the CWC deroutinized higher education and, as such, made us important to the college. Our value came from resisting and challenging the norm, from opening access for people who did not see themselves as writers, from creating forums for public expression by overlooked community members. President Bioteau said, "The Community Writing Center speaks to a . . . [deep] root of how community colleges even came to exist: to provide access to higher education, of course, but . . . also to provide community literacy towards the support of democracy." As we drafted our arguments against moving the CWC, we remembered and recognized what the center was before it was a place: it was an effort to make change.

Though the origin of the CWC was a tactical one, to return to this origin we had to become strategic. In doing so, we established institutional policies and structures that would assert the CWC's power in relationship with other organizations. Capitalizing on the college's resources, we worked with the Institutional Assessment Office to develop outcomes and measurements to document tactical work. This was not a return to the failed Writing Partners application process wherein we assumed partners would jump through hoops to be granted access to the CWC's "resources." Instead we established systematic guidelines through which we would enter into partnership, guidelines that would require us to disrupt socioeconomic privilege. At the same time, we realized that we no longer controlled the "place" of the Community Writing Center; its physical site belonged to both the college and the middle-class community. Therefore, following a rhetoric of respect for the desires of these communities, programs that took place at the center's location (e.g., Writing Coaching, workshops, writing groups that met there) would continue to be guided by that shared ownership—we would not contest the literacies that evolved there.

However, the Writing Partners program, a program not bounded by place, underwent a significant revision. In the year following the budget crisis, all potential partnerships were evaluated on a three-point scale:

1. Does the project/partnership work with underserved, underrepresented, or vulnerable populations?
2. Does the project/partnership provide opportunities for practical or activist writing (writing for change)?
3. Does the project/partnership provide ways for students of any grade level (elementary, high school, or college) to engage with writing?

Only projects that met at least two of the three criteria would be considered for partnership unless CWC resources were available to include others. This boundary established an internal range of tolerance for CWC partnerships. During the following year, the CWC entered into collaborations with the center for homeless youth, the county jail system, a children's hospital, and the YWCA. This strategy controlled with whom the Community Writing Center would enter into relationship, but it did not alter the tactical ways the CWC engaged inside of relationships: following a rhetoric of respect to capitalize on immediate resources and using time in clever ways, all to shake the webs of regulation. Though the selection of partnerships was now strategically conducted, within them a collaborative dance took place, with the organization identifying the kind of change they sought, rather than the CWC determining it for them.

CONCLUSION: RESPECT AND CHANGE

I have come to appreciate the complex interplay between strategic and tactical engagement, between institutional and deroutinizing purposes. Efforts to deviate from the norm require constant pivoting through acclimation and disruption, disruption and acclimation. Becoming wedded to either would have led to the demise of change that the Community Writing Center sought: the potential for people to pivot into a "writer" identity, asserting agency with their own textual choices within discursive environments. Disruption will inevitably meet the boundaries of the norm's tolerances: writers may assert agency and make choices, but if they wish to vibrate the web of a discursive environment, they must acknowledge and respond to the norm. Still, acclimating to the norm for too long and in too many ways subsumes agency and choice into the web—and change stops. Perhaps the goal is a balancing act that takes place in what Stephen Parks might term *counterspaces* that direct their efforts toward challenging the "common sense" within higher education and community (xxiv).

While I cofounded and directed the Community Writing Center, the CWC writing assistants and faculty directors, advisory committees, volunteers, writers, and partner organizations shared energy to create a particular environment of sustainability and disruption, the outcomes of which are hopeful and uncertain at the same time. The SLCC Community Writing Center continues working within the Salt Lake community, and several universities and colleges have opened community writing centers in the past few years—the University of New Mexico's Albuquerque Community Writing Center, Auburn University's Community Writing Center, and Utah Valley

University's Community Writing Center, to name a few. This kind of commitment to community writing centers represents some kind of shift in how academic institutions relate to people living in the communities that surround them.

And yet such change is quite small considering the vast ecosystems in which the Community Writing Center enacted a different vision of literacy education: community and higher education. Environments like those at the CWC tend to hang on tenaciously due to the dedication of people who inhabit them. As Norton and Goldblatt write, "Many programs are sustained by the dedicated work of a small cadre of individuals, any of whose sudden absence could lead to the demise of a program" (44). All that the Community Writing Center became could suddenly end—for example, if a new president didn't recognize its relevance to the college's mission—because disruptive programs like the CWC exist at the intersection of possibility and cessation; in the institutional space of higher education, they are always optional. To become an essential element in higher education, as student writing centers have in many ways managed to do,[17] a community writing center would likely have to mutate into a very different being.

But the range of tolerance for a community writing center is large enough for disruption if we are open to flexible definitions of what change can be. It can reside in the "'gaps' and 'fissures' of the social terrain in order to support 'alternative' alliances and collective possibilities" (Parks 32). In the SLCC Community Writing Center's development, Ruffus and I found just that: a gap inside of which to pivot between our identities as college educators and as community members, a gap that required relationships, patience, effort, and acceptance of different notions of change—momentary, temporal, individual, and collective. Similarly, Dobrin and Weisser write of students in composition classrooms:

> We can only hope to enable the students we come in contact with at least once a week to become more critical of the world around them and more efficient producers of writing. And we cannot expect to make changes in more than a few of their lives each semester. But what we must not overlook is the

individual lives that we stand a very good chance of affecting in our classrooms and, in turn, how those lives will encounter others. (109)

The kind of change that Dobrin and Weisser are arguing for here, I believe, is one that develops within a rhetoric of respect. It is a respect for the people we enter into relationship with, both those we hope to empower and those we partner with in the process. It is respect for the wholeness of the life that each person brings to our relationships and for the relationships those individuals have with others. It is a respect for the importance of change, no matter how big or small, nor how it may be defined. Finally, it is a respect for the resources and limitations that we each bring to making change, acknowledging what we each can and cannot do and what our energies may create together. The SLCC Community Writing Center resisted the web of literacy education in Salt Lake City to establish itself. It then shook the web and built new strands on the system's edges. Since that time, people, organizations, and even institutions have reached out from those new strands to make their own change—change that is recognized, even if only by the people making it.

Preface

1. Although, as of the time of writing, the CWC is still operating as a vital part of SLCC and the Salt Lake community, my inquiry is limited to the years I was there—1998 to 2010—and therefore is written in the past tense. I do this to ensure that the interpretations and analyses herein are understood as mine alone. Other people who are or have been in relationship with the SLCC Community Writing Center may derive very different meanings from it than I have done. At the same time, I use the generic pronoun *we* frequently throughout this book. Because the CWC was such a collaborative environment, with dozens of people contributing to its life, it is not possible for me to write about it exclusively in the first person. Choices were made collectively, so *we* is most often appropriate, though I try to note when a specific individual, including myself, was primarily responsible for an activity or decision.
2. See Devet and Gillam for two examples of ecological approaches to writing center work.
3. Conveniently, my past (and current) relationship and experiences with the CWC have primed me for some of the parenting challenges I face with my (human) son, who was born four years after the CWC was established.

1. Recognizing the SLCC Community Writing Center

1. See Deans.
2. See Flower, Long, and Higgins's *Learning to Rival*.
3. See Parks and Goldblatt.
4. See Deans, Roswell, and Wurr; Long; and Rose and Weiser.
5. As of this writing, the UWM Community Writing Assistance program has been undergoing a shift to use community volunteers trained by graduate students so that it can provide more tutoring days and times to the community.

6. See Abels, Clemens, Wilson, Winters, and Woods's "'Here in This Place': Write On! of Durham, North Carolina."

7. See Rousculp, "Connecting the Community and the Center."

8. See Guest.

9. See Case, Knepler, and Soni.

10. See Mathieu, Parks, and Rousculp.

11. See Boquet's *Noise from the Writing Center.*

12. All writers' names and identifying information have been changed unless otherwise noted.

13. Salt Lake City is home to thousands of refugees from around the world because it is one of the initial resettlement cities for the US government refugee program.

14. All participants in CWC programs were referred to as "writers," and I have used this term throughout this book.

15. The DWS publication's title, *sine cera,* derived from the Latin concept "without wax," which described sculptures that had not had their imperfections filled in with wax. See Rousculp, "When the Community Writes."

16. See Rousculp, "When the Community Writes."

17. In the final chapter, I examine the decreased ethnic diversity and increased income and education levels of CWC writers.

18. The director taught two classes a year and the assistant director—which later became associate director—taught four and tutored in the writing center. Both had the same committee and departmental/college service assignments as any other faculty member.

19. Until 2007, a blend of academics and community members served on just one advisory committee. When an external review revealed frustration with academic cliques, we decided to split in two. At the time, it felt like we had failed to bridge higher education and community participation, even though both groups functioned much better with their distinct purposes and discourses. Eventually we realized that while the CWC balanced between academic and community environments, the bodies that supported it didn't need to.

20. Although immigrant laborers arrived from many countries, the Greek and Japanese populations dominated due to the efforts of Leonidas Skliris from Greece and Daigoro Hashimoto from Japan. See "Immigration."

21. With the exception of the cities of Salt Lake, Price, and Moab, most population centers (and rural areas) across the state are predominantly LDS.

2. Evolving a Discursive Ecology: A Rhetoric of Respect

1. See "Dropout": nationally, only 72.7 percent of students of Hispanic/Latino origins graduated from high school in 2009, whereas 93.5 percent of White students did. Also see *Literacy as a Civil Right* edited by Stuart Greene.

2. See Gee, "Literacy, Discourse, and Linguistics."

3. See Jordan.

4. USC's commitment to its surrounding neighborhood is outlined on their website: http://communities.usc.edu.

5. Summer Beginnings: Summer Youth and Employment Training Program Training Manual, 1994.

6. Paulo Freire wrote, "It would be extremely naïve to expect the dominant classes to develop a type of education that would enable the subordinate classes to perceive social injustice critically" (*Pedagogy of the Oppressed* 102). I was naïve.

7. After the CWC opened, English faculty member Allison Fernley led the Artspace Writing Project during its final year of production.

8. For example, see Herzberg.

9. Graciously, Susan Miller served on the CWC's Steering Committee and then on the Advisory Committee for several years.

10. Years after the CWC opened, when it began to draw attention from other institutions and faculty interested in community writing projects, we were often approached for advice on how to get new projects started. In these situations, rarely had they spoken with their campus writing centers to ask for support, or if they had, the writing center typically responded with "student-only" limitations.

11. See Lunsford.

12. See also Boquet (*Noise*); Carino; Ferruci and DeRosa; Lerner; Pemberton and Kinkead; and Parks (42–44).

13. Ultimately, I cannot explain how or why the college decided to go ahead with the CWC; two administrators, not Ruffus or I, made it happen and kept it alive. Only eighteen months after the CWC opened, the same president who approved the initial budget for the CWC put the center on the chopping block—the first budget cut in response to the college's financial hardship. In a response coordinated by Brugger, six deans and division chairs from around the college took money out of their own budgets to save the CWC. That's something only an administrator with power can do.

14. See Abels et al.; Coogan ("Sophists"); Goldblatt; Jacobi; and Parks.

3. Transforming Energy in Pursuit of Uncertainty

1. See Gardner, "Effects."
2. Nearly 46 percent of registered writers at the CWC had their bachelor's or advanced degrees.
3. Cumulative results from six years of anonymous workshop evaluations indicated that knowledge of the "teacher" or "facilitator" was one of the two main elements cited in the positive feedback. The other was the collaborative environment the facilitator created.
4. See Ellen Cushman's "Sustainable Service Learning Programs."
5. Further contributing to these discourses was the center's open design: our constant face-to-face presence leveled power differences and eliminated the possibility of disengaging from one another.
6. Like small nonprofits, we did our own janitorial and cleaning work, occasional painting, and some small repair.
7. Current education statistics show that while masses of students work their way successfully through their college educations, great numbers of students who start out in college do not finish. Nationally, about 58 percent of full-time students at four-year institutions graduate in six years, but the rate is less than 40 percent for Black students and averages 49 percent for Hispanic students (National Center for Education Statistics). Even fewer students persist beyond a bachelor's degree into advanced or graduate work.
8. The role of the community college system as a "cooling out" or "diversionary" institution in the management of educational aspirations has been debated for years. A 2002 study on community college student transfer to any four-year institution within five years of leaving the community college shows a range of 25–52 percent based on the pool of students being studied (Wellman). The low end of the range is an average across all students in the study; the high end is students enrolled in an academic major taking courses toward a bachelor's degree.
9. See Bruffee ("Collaborative," "Peer"); Cushman (*Struggle*); Denny; Flower (*Community*, "Going," "Intercultural," "RE: What Does"); Goldblatt ("Alinsky's," *Because*); Grabill; Harris ("Using"); Lerner; Mathieu; North; Parks; and Pemberton and Kinkead, among others.
10. I do not mean to suggest that deferring to faculty authority is a negative trait of academic environments. In fact, writing program administrators and academic administrators paying heed to this authority is at the heart of academic freedom policies. My mention of it in this context is to illustrate the discursive ideology that aca-

demic writing centers must respond to by existing within academic environments.

11. Including Murphy and Sherwood; Capossela; Gillespie and Lerner; Ryan and Zimmerelli; Rafoth.

12. This is perhaps another way of describing Freire's "banking" concept of education.

13. See Geisler (33) and Ellsworth, *Teaching* (47).

14. Geisler argues that the long exposure students receive in K–12 education to the primacy of the autonomous text is a significant factor in the struggle many students experience in introductory composition courses that expect them to be able to navigate rhetorically within texts.

15. A play on a prison term for making do with something else when the real thing isn't available.

16. Hypocritically, there was one workshop I was never able to hand over to the writing assistants: a three-month "Introduction to Grant Writing" workshop that we provided in collaboration with a state arts agency. Whether because of the workshop's depth, length, or "professional" collaboration, writing assistants sat in on the workshop and served as writing team facilitators for the participants but were never allowed to lead it.

17. When the Olympics came to Salt Lake City, the collector pin trading phenomenon also arrived, with shops selling out of hundreds of different "Salt Lake 2002" pins—the most-prized of which was the "Utah Green Jello" pin, a delicacy humorously associated with LDS cuisine.

4. Shifting Relations, Transforming Expectations

1. In our exchange, Flower wasn't cautioning me regarding the CWC's intentions. Rather, her comments were made in response to a question I posed regarding how I might measure the CWC's success.

2. Several assessments of the DWS program have demonstrated that long-term participation results in increased levels of confidence in writing ability, motivation to write, and appreciation for diversity.

3. See Cushman, "Sustainable"; Goldblatt, *Because* 54–55; Mathieu.

4. Jeffrey Grabill's critique of literacy programs speaks directly to such contradictions.

5. In 2008 the CWC's assessment practices were included in the Writing Program Administrator's "Assessment Gallery and Resources—Assessment Models and Communication Strategies," http://wpa council.org/assessment-models/.

6. See Mathieu and Goldblatt, "Alinsky's," for discussions of conversation.
7. Such an emphasis is not limited to rhetoric. As John Ackerman and David Coogan point out, "The discourse of service and civic engagement is on the rise at our colleges and universities as policies and practices that identify service learning, the scholarship of engagement, community outreach, public consultancy, and public intellectualism as the work before us to do" ("Introduction" 1).
8. See Appendix B for the evolution of the CWC's mission statements.
9. For an extensive description and analysis of these methods, see Flower, Long, and Higgins's *Learning to Rival*.
10. See Nancy Fraser.
11. Many years later, in an attempted partnership with a health care reform nonprofit, the CWC developed a series of workshops and Writing Coaching projects to gather stories from people who were uninsured or underinsured. Together we were certain that people would flood this project with their stories, based on the verbal complaints that were freely shared in small focus groups conducted before the start of the program. In the end, even though anonymity was an option for the writers, not a single story was submitted throughout the entire six months of the project.
12. Such restrictions exist in academic environments too. Harry Denny writes, "By becoming more aware of the codes constituting their identities and the codes' implications for academic life, students gain a modicum of agency. However, that sense of empowerment is always confounded by dominant interests' resistance to challenges to the status quo. Knowledge of and being able to act on codes does not diminish the reality and effect of their existence when these codes privilege certain ways of writing and speaking over others" (45).
13. "No matter how good it might feel to imagine ourselves more central, believing ourselves to be central is the ultimate trick hegemony plays" (Parks 68).
14. At one point, we were asked by a writing group in the DiverseCity Writing Series to indicate in the *sine cera* anthology which writers were from which groups in order to distinguish the more in-depth and "advanced" writers from those in groups serving more disenfranchised populations. We adamantly disagreed with this proposal for just that reason; we were committed to ensuring that all of the writers were seen as writers, without an identification of good, bad, advanced, literate, illiterate, whatever.

15. After she presented the concerns to the organization, she did receive a written apology for their actions.

5. Engaging Place: Acclimation and Disruption

1. Although such work takes place in both community colleges and four-year colleges as well, Mathieu's work focuses on university–community relationships.
2. From the Latin to "lead, bring, take, draw."
3. Over the course of the year prior to the fundraiser, the college's marketing department decided that all advertising, public service announcements, handouts, publications, and other materials regarding the center had to include the name "SLCC Community Writing Center." In the years before that, we used simply the "Community Writing Center" in such media, with the connection to the college made verbally and through relationships. This was intentional, to avoid barriers related to the issue of who belongs in a "higher education" space. After the CWC had achieved a level of recognition in the community, the college understandably mandated that "SLCC" be clearly and publicly established as the institutional home of the center.
4. Perhaps only I was overwhelmed with anxiety regarding the outcome of the meeting. At its end, after President Bioteau had left, Stephen Goldsmith, founder of Artspace and chair of the CWC Community Advisory Committee, asked me, "Where do you want to be a year from now?" Realizing that this particular fight for the survival of the CWC was the last one I had in me (there had been so many during the previous decade), I blurted out, "Not here." At that moment I knew I would leave the Community Writing Center; my time with it was coming to an end.
5. See Ellsworth, *Places.*
6. Community colleges are sometimes publicly represented as educationally inferior to four-year colleges or universities, as in popular culture references like the television series *Community* (2009–present). This perception, combined with the image of colleges and universities as centers of intellectual life, can result in some members of the public believing that a community college cannot provide valuable educational opportunities to them.
7. NPR ended its *This I Believe* series in 2009; it can now be found on the Web at www.thisibelieve.org.
8. NPR Audience Insight and Research, "NPR Profile 2009: Insights into the Public Radio Audience," www.wqub.org WQUB Radio,

April 22, 2011, and "Audience," National Public Radio, npr.org, April 22, 2011.

9. See Girlswritenow.org.

10. SLCC Community Writing Center/SLC Library "Salt Lake Girls Write" Partnership Proposal Draft. 14 Sep. 2009.

11. That exchange with Meads was the confirming sign for me that the SLCC Community Writing Center had "grown beyond" me as its founding director. With it, I knew that my decision to leave was the right one.

12. It should be noted that after I left the CWC, at the directive of the City Library the program changed to "Salt Lake Teens Write" to include boys and subsequently received an SLCC innovation award in its second year of operation.

13. Much later in *Tactics of Hope*, Mathieu writes, "Clearly, predictability, continuity, and funded positions and spaces can benefit service-learning programs a great deal. Scholars . . . make compelling cases for the advantage that institutionalized and long-term service-learning projects can yield. My concern, however, is that we must also consider the disadvantages of institutionalized models and consider more local *tactical* options as well" (96). See Paul Feigenbaum's "Tactics and Strategies of Relationship-Based Practice."

14. "SLCC Community Writing Center Working Proposal 'Template,'" 22 Feb. 2000.

15. Such an intended outcome is not uncommon; see, particularly, the nationally recognized University Neighborhood Partners program at the University of Utah.

16. The percentage of writers who had not attained a high school diploma or GED annually ranged between 2.0 and 6.3 percent. The cumulative average was 3.3 percent of all writers registered with the CWC.

17. Yet student writing centers are also subject to critiques of acclimation and colonization; see Bawarshi and Pelkowski.

APPENDIX A

APPENDIX A

Foundational Principles of the
SLCC Community Writing Center
2006

Opened in October 2001, the SLCC Community Writing Center is based on principles of Education, Community and Collaboration. These principles should serve as a framework for the future of the CWC, further, **the CWC has historically challenged—and should continue to challenge—the following assumptions about writing and education:**

- That some types of writing are more valuable than others,
- That publication validates a piece of writing,
- That higher education is somehow separate from community education, and
- That higher education can know what a community needs or wants without entering into full and mutually-beneficial partnership with that community.

Education: The CWC is a place . . .

- Of learning: all CWC activities are developed for people to gain literacy skills, knowledge and/or abilities they did not have before.
- For student employees to learn to become teachers, mentors, developers and managers. Students should always be a part of the CWC staff and special efforts should be made to recruit student employees from SLCC.
- Where effective writers develop through the responses of skilled readers; CWC Writing Assistants are skilled readers.
- Where programming maintains a balance across all types of writing (practical, civic and personal).

Community: The CWC and its programs . . .

- Must be available to everyone, regardless of income, education, ethnicity, opinion or background.

- Do not duplicate already existing writing services or programs; rather the CWC coordinates with other organizations to mutual benefit.

- Actively seek out partnerships with communities and individuals who have been traditionally-underserved by higher education.

Collaboration: The CWC believes that . . .

- Because all writing is, at some point, a collaborative act, the CWC is a collaborative environment on all levels.

- Collaborations should always be guided by our partner in learning and focused on developing new writing knowledge.

- Our programming should be responsive to community requests and inquiries; the CWC does not determine what the community's writing needs and desires are.

- We should not take any political or philosophical position in a writing partnership; rather we focus on writing instruction only.

APPENDIX B

SLCC Community Writing Center Mission Statements

2001

The Community Writing Center (CWC) is the community outreach branch of the Salt Lake Community College Writing Program. At the CWC, we believe that proficient and flexible writing abilities are essential resources to reach personal and professional goals and to participate fully in our community. Our mission is to provide the opportunity to improve, expand, and refine these resources for all individuals and organizations in Salt Lake City.

We base this mission on the following assumptions:

- People—individually and in community—can use writing to discover and understand their lives, relationships, shared interests and purposes.

- Writing effectively, insightfully and productively across diverse writing situations can empower individuals and the communities to which they belong.

- Writing is one of the many resources an individual uses to express, to communicate, and to achieve personal and professional goals. Individuals can bridge from existing resources and literate abilities to new ones with effort and capable assistance.

- Writing is one form of sharing our life stories and experiences with others, and has the potential to humanize our community, increase appreciation of diversity, and improve acceptance of difference.

- Educational institutions have a responsibility to respond to the needs of their communities by providing learning situations for individuals and organizations outside of the traditional educational structure.

To fulfill this mission the CWC strives to bring together—and collaborate with—working alliances among individuals and educational, community, for-profit, non-profit and governmental organizations to develop learning programs, projects and community partnerships. The CWC provides writing assistance and resources to individuals, organizations and businesses through one-on-one tutoring, short-term and extended workshops, and outreach programs. We also provide substantive service-learning opportunities for SLCC and other college-level students and volunteer opportunities for the Salt Lake general public.

2002

Because writing effectively is a means to improving people's lives, the mission of the SLCC Community Writing Center is to support the writing goals of out-of-school adults. We fulfill this mission by initiating and developing short and long term writing programs and projects and by collaborating with working alliances to identify ways that our resources can serve the community. The CWC also provides training and opportunities for college students and the general public to contribute to our mission.

We undertake this with the following assumptions about education, writing and community:

1. Quality education should provide alternative and on-going learning opportunities to the communities it serves . . . AND Individuals and organizations should be active participants in the education of their communities.

2. Writing effectively supports the ability of individuals and organizations to participate in their communities and to reach personal and professional goals . . . AND Writing with advice and response from others is a way to become an effective writer.

3. Successful urban communities have thoughtful conversations about social and economic quality, acceptance of diversity, and peaceful relations . . . AND Thoughtful writing for others is one important way to promote these conversations.

2005

The SLCC Community Writing Center promotes the improvement of writing abilities for personal, economic and social goals. To achieve this mission, the CWC sponsors innovative outreach programs and collaborates with community partners to identify the best use of its educational resources.

2006–2010
Everybody can write! The SLCC Community Writing Center supports, motivates and educates people of all abilities and educational backgrounds who want to use writing for practical needs, civic engagement and personal expression.

REFERENCES

826national.org. 826 National, n.d. Web. 29 Sept. 2010.

Abels, Kimberly, Kristina Moore Clemens, Julie Wilson, Autumn Winters, and Mahogany Woods. "'Here in This Place': Write On! of Durham, North Carolina." Mathieu, Parks, and Rousculp 133–50.

Ackerman, John M. "Rhetorical Engagement in the Cultural Economies of Cities." Ackerman and Coogan 76–97.

Ackerman, John M., and David J. Coogan. "Introduction: The Space to Work in Public Life." Ackerman and Coogan 1–18.

Ackerman, John M., and David J. Coogan, eds. *The Public Work of Rhetoric: Citizen-Scholars and Civic Engagement.* Columbia: U of South Carolina P, 2010. Print.

Adler-Kassner, Linda. *The Activist WPA: Changing Stories about Writing and Writers.* Logan: Utah State UP, 2008. Print.

Allison, Mike, and Jude Kaye. "Characteristics of Nonprofit Organizations—Implications for Consultation." Mar. 2003. Web. 11 Jan. 2011.

"Artspace Bridge Projects." *ArtspaceUtah.org.* Artspace, 2010. Web. 21 Oct. 2010.

Artz, Lee. "Speaking Truth to Power: Observations from Experience." Kahn and Lee 47–55.

Bawarshi, Anis. "The Ecology of Genre." Weisser and Dobrin 69–80.

Bawarshi, Anis, and Stephanie Pelkowski. "Postcolonialism and the Idea of a Writing Center." *Writing Center Journal* 19.2 (1999): 41–58. Print.

Bazerman, Charles. "The Work of a Middle-Class Activist: Stuck in History." Kahn and Lee 37–46.

Bergmann, Linda S. "The Writing Center as a Site of Engagement." Rose and Weiser 160–76.

Bioteau, Cynthia. Personal Interview. 1 June 2011.

Boquet, Elizabeth H. *Noise from the Writing Center.* Logan: Utah State UP, 2002. Print.

———. "'Our Little Secret': A History of Writing Centers, Pre- to Post-Open Admissions." *CCC* 50.3 (1999): 463–82. Print.

Brandt, Deborah. "Literacy in American Lives: Living and Learning in a Sea of Change." *Literacy and Learning: Reflections on Writing, Reading, and Society.* By Brandt. San Francisco: Wiley, 2009. 47–65. Print.

———. "Sponsors of Literacy." *CCC* 49. 2. (1998): 165–85. Print.

Bruffee, Kenneth A. "Collaborative Learning and the 'Conversation of Mankind.'" *College English* 46. 7 (1984): 635–52. Print.

———. "Peer Tutoring and the 'Conversation of Mankind.'" Olson 3–15.

Capossela, Toni-Lee. *The Harcourt Brace Guide to Peer Tutoring.* Fort Worth: Harcourt, 1998. Print.

Caputo, John, and Mark Yount. " Institutions, Normalization, and Power." Introduction. *Foucault and the Critique of Institutions.* Ed. Caputo and Yount. University Park: Pennsylvania State UP, 1993. 3–26. Print.

Carino, Peter. "Open Admissions and the Construction of Writing Center History: A Tale of Three Models." *The Writing Center Journal* 17.1 (1996): 30–48. Print.

Case, Mairead, Annie Knepler, and Rupal Soni. "Sharing Space: Collaborative Programming within and between Communities." Mathieu, Parks, and Rousculp 150–62.

Certeau, Michel de. *The Practice of Everyday Life.* Trans. Steven Rendall. Berkeley: U of California P, 1984. Print.

Christiansen, Ron. "Belief(s) in SLC: Writing through Differences: Final Summary Report." 13 May 2005. TS.

Cintron, Ralph. "Democracy and its Limitations." Ackerman and Coogan 98–118.

Cloud, Dana L. "The Only Conceivable Thing to Do: Reflections on Academics and Activism." Kahn and Lee 11–24.

Commoner, Barry. *The Closing Circle: Nature, Man, and Technology.* New York: Knopf, 1971. Print.

Community Literacy Center (CSU). Colorado State U, n.d. Web. 27 Oct. 2010.

Coogan, David. "David Coogan—Prison Writing Workshop at the Richmond City Jail." *David Coogan,* 2009. Web. 12 Jan. 2011.

———. "Sophists for Social Change." Ackerman and Coogan 157–74.

Cooper, Ginger. "Building a Community around the Writing Center." *Praxis: A Writing Center Journal* 2.1 (2004): n. pag. Web. 2 Feb. 2005.

Cooper, Marilyn. "The Ecology of Writing." *College English* 48.4 (1986): 364–75. Print.

Cundiff, H. Lynn. Personal Interview. 2 Apr. 2002.

Cushman, Ellen. "The Rhetorician as an Agent of Social Change." *CCC* 47.1 (1996): 7–28. Print.

————. *The Struggle and the Tools: Oral and Literate Strategies in an Inner City Community.* Albany: State U of New York P, 1998. Print.

————. "Sustainable Service Learning Programs." *CCC* 54.1 (2002): 40–65. Print.

Davidson, Lee, and Molly Farmer. "Utah 10th for Percentage of Budget Spent on Education." *Deseret News* 15 July 2010. Web. 20 Sept. 2010.

Deans, Thomas. *Writing Partnerships: Service-Learning in Composition.* Urbana, IL: NCTE, 2000. Print.

Deans, Thomas, Barbara Roswell, and Adrian Wurr, eds. *Writing and Community Engagement: A Critical Sourcebook.* Boston: Bedford/St. Martin's, 2010. Print.

Denny, Harry. "Queering the Writing Center." *Writing Center Journal* 25:2 (2005): 39–62. Print.

Devet, Bonnie D. "Redefining the Writing Center with Ecocomposition." *Composition Forum* 23 (2011): n. pag. Web. 7 May 2012.

Dobrin, Sidney I., and Christian R. Weisser. *Natural Discourse: Toward Ecocomposition.* Albany: SUNY P, 2002. Print.

Doggart, Julia, Melissa Tedrowe, and Kate Viera. "Minding the Gap: Realizing Our Ideal Community Writing Center." *Community Literacy Journal* 1.2 (2007): 71–80. Print.

Drew, Julie. "The Politics of Place: Student Travelers and Pedagogical Maps. Weisser and Dobrin 57–68.

"Dropout and Completion Rates in the United States: 2007—National Status Completion Rates." *National Center for Education Statistics.* NCES, 23 Sept. 2009. Web. 27 Oct. 2010.

Ellsworth, Elizabeth. *Places of Learning: Media, Architecture, Pedagogy.* New York: Routledge, 2005. Print.

————. *Teaching Positions: Difference, Pedagogy, and the Power of Address.* New York: Teachers College P, 1997. Print.

Farmer, Molly, and Lee Davidson. "Utah Last in Spending per Pupil— Again." *Deseret News* 29 June 2010. Web. 20 Sept. 2010.

Feigenbaum, Paul. "Tactics and Strategies of Relationship-Based Practice: Reassessing the Institutionalization of Community Literacy." *Community Literacy Journal* 5.2 (2011): 47–66. Print.

Ferruci, Stephen, and Susan DeRosa. "Writing a Sustainable History: Mapping Writing Center Ethos." Murphy and Stay 21–32.

Flower, Linda. *Community Literacy and the Rhetoric of Public Engagement.* Carbondale: Southern Illinois UP, 2008. Print.

————. "Going Public—in a Disabling Discourse." Ackerman and Coogan 137–56.

———. "Intercultural Inquiry and the Transformation of Service." *College English* 65.2 (2002): 181–201. Print.

———. "RE: What Does CWC Have to Tell Us?" Message to the author. 12 Nov. 2008. Email.

Flower, Linda, and John R. Hayes. "The Cognition of Discovery: Defining a Rhetorical Problem." *CCC* 31.1 (1980): 21–32. Print.

Flower, Linda, and Shirley Brice Heath. "Drawing on the Local: Collaboration and Community Expertise." *Language and Learning across the Disciplines* 4.3 (Oct. 2000): 43–55. Print.

Flower, Linda, Elenore Long, and Lorraine Higgins. *Learning to Rival: A Literate Practice for Intercultural Inquiry.* Mahwah, NJ: Erlbaum, 2000. Print.

Fraser, Nancy. "Rethinking the Public Sphere: A Contribution to the Critique of Actually Existing Democracy." *Social Text* 25/26 (1990): 56–80. Print.

Freire, Paulo. *Education for Critical Consciousness.* New York: Seabury, 1973. Print.

———. *Pedagogy of Hope: Reliving Pedagogy of the Oppressed.* Trans. Robert R. Barr. New York: Continuum, 1994. Print.

———. *Pedagogy of the Oppressed.* 30th anniversary ed. Trans. Myra Bergman Ramos. New York: Continuum, 2009. Print.

Gardner, Clinton. "The Effects of Working as a Peer Tutor on Community College Students." International Writing Centers Association/National Conference on Peer Tutoring Joint Conference. Baltimore, Maryland. 4 Nov. 2010. Conference Presentation.

Gee, James Paul. "Literacy, Discourse, and Linguistics: Introduction *and* What Is Literacy?" *Literacy: A Critical Sourcebook.* Ed. Ellen Cushman, Eugene R. Kintgen, Barry M. Kroll, and Mike Rose. Boston: Bedford/St. Martin's, 2001. 525–44. Print.

Geisler, Cheryl. *Academic Literacy and the Nature of Expertise: Reading, Writing and Knowing in Academic Philosophy.* Hillsdale, NJ: Erlbaum, 1994. Print.

Geller, Anne Ellen, Michele Eodice, Frankie Condon, Meg Carroll, and Elizabeth H. Boquet. *The Everyday Writing Center: A Community of Practice.* Logan: Utah State UP, 2007. Print.

George, Diana. "The Word on the Street: Public Discourse in a Culture of Disconnect." *Reflections* 2.2 (2002): 6–18. Print.

George, Diana, and Paula Mathieu. "A Place for the Dissident Press in Rhetorical Education: 'Sending Up a Signal Flare in the Darkness.'" Ackerman and Coogan 247–66.

Gill, Judy. "In-house Tutor Handbooks and the Problem of Negative Rhetoric." *Writing Lab Newsletter* 35.5/6 (2011): 11–13. Print.

Gillam, Alice M. "Writing Center Ecology: A Bakhtinian Perspective." *Writing Center Journal* 11.2 (1991): 3–11. Print.

Gillespie, Paula, and Neal Lerner. *The Longman Guide to Peer Tutoring.* 2nd ed. New York: Longman, 2007. Print.

"Girls Write Now—Welcome." *Girlswritenow.org.* Girls Write Now, n.d. Web. 27 Mar. 2010.

Goldblatt, Eli. "Alinsky's Reveille: A Community-Organizing Model for Neighborhood-Based Literacy Projects." *College English* 67.3 (2005): 274–95. Print.

———. *Because We Live Here: Sponsoring Literacy beyond the College Curriculum.* Cresskill, NJ: Hampton, 2007. Print.

Goldblatt, Eli, with Manuel Portillo and Mark Lyons. "Story to Action: A Conversation about Literacy and Organizing." *Community Literacy* 2.2 (2008): 45–66. Print.

Grabill, Jeffrey T. *Community Literacy Programs and the Politics of Change.* Albany: State U of New York P, 2001. Print.

Greene, Stuart, ed. *Literacy as a Civil Right: Reclaiming Social Justice in Literacy Teaching and Learning.* New York: Lang, 2008. Print.

Guest, Sara, with Hanna Neuschwander and Robyn Steely. "Respect, Writing, Community: Write Around Portland." Mathieu, Parks, and Rousculp 49–70.

Hadfield, Leslie, Joyce Kinkead, Tom C. Peterson, Stephanie H. Ray, and Sarah S. Preston. "An Ideal Writing Center: Re-imagining Space and Design." Pemberton and Kinkead 166–75.

Harris, Muriel. "SLATE (Support for the Learning and Teaching of English) Statement: The Concept of the Writing Center." *International Writing Centers Association.* IWCA, 2006. Web. 11 July 2010.

———. "Using Tutorial Principles to Train Tutors: Practicing our Praxis." Murphy and Stay 301–10.

Hauser, Gerard A. Foreword. Ackerman and Coogan ix–xii.

Haviland, Carol Peterson, Carmen M. Fye, and Richard Colby. "The Politics of Administrative and Physical Location." *The Politics of Writing Centers.* Ed. Jane Nelson and Kathy Evertz. Portsmouth, NH: Boynton/Cook, 2001. 85–98. Print.

Hayashi, Reiko, and Tiffany Rousculp. "The 'Our Homes, Not Nursing Homes' Project: Lives of People with Disabilities in Nursing Homes." *Journal of Social Work in Disability and Rehabilitation* 3.2 (2004): 57–70. Print.

Heath, Shirley Brice. *Ways with Words: Language, Life, and Work in Communities and Classrooms.* New York: Cambridge UP, 1983. Print.

Herzberg, Bruce. "Community Service and Critical Teaching." *CCC* 45.3 (1994): 307–19. Print.

hooks, bell. *Yearning: Race, Gender, and Cultural Politics.* Boston: South End, 1990. Print.

Horning, Alice. "The History and Role of Libraries in Adult Literacy." *Community Literacy Journal* 5.1 (2010): 151–72. Print.

"Immigration of Utah's Foreign-Born Population (1860–1980)." Utah Education Network. Web. 22 Sept. 2013.

"Institute for the Study of Literature, Literacy, and Culture." *ISLLC.* Temple U, 1999. Web. 1 Jan. 2000.

Jacobi, Tobi. "Slipping Pages through Razor Wire: Literacy Action Projects in Jail." *Community Literacy Journal* 2.2 (2008): 67–86. Print.

Jones, Charisse. "USC Dream Team: Students Become Scholars in Novel Program." *Los Angeles Times* 19 July 1992. Print.

Jordan, June. "Nobody Mean More to Me than You and the Future Life of Willie Jordan." *On Call: Political Essays.* By Jordan. New York: South End, 1985. 123–40. Print.

Kahn, Seth, and JongHwa Lee. *Activism and Rhetoric: Theories and Contexts for Political Engagement.* New York: Routledge, 2011. Print.

Lerner, Neal. *The Idea of a Writing Laboratory.* Carbondale: Southern Illinois UP, 2009. Print.

Long, Elenore. *Community Literacy and the Rhetoric of Local Publics.* West Lafayette, IN: Parlor, 2008. Print.

Lunsford, Andrea. "Collaboration, Control and the Idea of a Writing Center." *Writing Center Journal* 12.1 (1991): 3–10. Print.

Lyons, Mark, and August Tarrier, eds. *Espejos y Ventanas: Historias Orales de Trabajadores Agrícolas Mexicanos y sus Familias (Mirrors and Windows: Oral Histories of Mexican Farmworkers and their Families).* Philadelphia: New City Community, 2004. Print.

Maclay, Kathleen. "UC Berkeley Literacy Program Attracts Oakland Youths, Seniors with Digital Storytelling." *UC Berkeley News Center.* U of California, 2 Dec. 2002. Web. 27 Oct. 2010.

Malouf, Andrea. Personal Interview. 18 Apr. 2011.

Mathieu, Paula. *Tactics of Hope: The Public Turn in English Composition.* Portsmouth, NH: Boynton/Cook, 2005. Print.

Mathieu, Paula, Stephen Parks, and Tiffany Rousculp, eds. *Circulating Communities: The Tactics and Strategies of Community Publishing.* Lanham, MD: Lexington, 2012.

Mattison, Michael. "Managing the Center: The Director as Coach." Murphy and Stay 93–102.

McQueen, Alisabeth. "CWC: A Place of Learning." *Community Writing Connection* 11.1 (2011): 1. Web.

Meads, Rachel. Personal Interview. 31 Aug. 2010.

Miller, Carolyn R. "Should We Name the Tools? Concealing and Revealing the Art of Rhetoric." Ackerman and Coogan 19–38.

Miller, Susan. "Language Alliances: A Public Literacy Center—Draft Prospectus." June 1997. Unpublished prospectus presented to U of Utah. TS.

Murphy, Christina, and Steve Sherwood. *The St. Martin's Sourcebook for Writing Tutors.* 2nd ed. Boston: Bedford/St. Martin's, 2003. Print.

Murphy, Christina, and Byron L. Stay, eds. *The Writing Center Director's Resource Book.* Mahwah, NJ: Erlbaum, 2006. Print.

National Center for Education Statistics. "Table 376. Percentage of First-Time Full-Time Bachelor's Degree-Seeking Students at 4-Year Institutions Who Completed a Bachelor's Degree, by Race/Ethnicity, Time to Completion, Sex, and Control of Institution: Selected Cohort Entry Years, 1996 through 2005." Nov. 2012. Web. 22 Sept. 2013.

Neighborhood Story Project. U of New Orleans, n.d. Web. 27 Oct. 2010.

"New City Press Mission Statement." *New City Community Press.* New City Community P, n.d. Web. 25 Apr. 2011.

"New York Writers Coalition—About." *NY Writers Coalition.* New York Writers Coalition, n.d. Web. 27 Oct. 2010.

North, Stephen M. "The Idea of a Writing Center." *College English* 46.5 (1984): 433–46. Print.

Norton, Michael H., and Eli Goldblatt. "Centering Community Literacy: The Art of Location within Institutions and Neighborhoods." Rose and Weiser 29–49.

Olson, Gary A., ed. *Writing Centers: Theory and Administration.* Urbana, IL: NCTE, 1984. Print.

Park, Judy W. "2009 Graduation and Dropout Rate Report—Revised." Utah State Office of Education. Department of Data, Assessment and Accountability. 16 Mar. 2010. Web. 19 Aug. 2010.

Parks, Stephen. *Gravyland: Writing Beyond the Curriculum in the City of Brotherly Love.* Syracuse: Syracuse UP, 2010. Print.

Parks, Steve, and Eli Goldblatt. "Writing beyond the Curriculum: Fostering New Collaborations in Literacy." *College English* 62.5 (2000): 584–606. Print.

Peck, Wayne Campbell, Linda Flower, and Lorraine Higgins. "Community Literacy." *CCC* 46.2 (1995): 199–222. Print.

Pemberton, Michael A., and Joyce Kinkead, eds. *The Center Will Hold: Critical Perspectives on Writing Center Scholarship*. Logan: Utah State UP, 2003. Print.

"Poverty Rate Rises in Utah." *KSL.com*. KSL Broadcasting, 29 Sep. 2010. Web. 27 Oct. 2010.

Rafoth, Ben, ed. *A Tutor's Guide: Helping Writers One to One*. 2nd ed. Portsmouth, NH: Boynton/Cook, 2005. Print.

Rose, Mike. *Lives on the Boundary: A Moving Account of the Struggles and Achievements of America's Educationally Underprepared*. New York: Penguin, 1989. Print.

———. *The Mind at Work: Valuing the Intelligence of the American Worker*. New York: Penguin, 2004. Print.

Rose, Shirley K., and Irwin Weiser, eds. *Going Public: What Writing Programs Learn from Engagement*. Logan: Utah State UP, 2010. Print.

Rousculp, Tiffany. "Connecting the Community and the Center: Service-Learning and Outreach." *Writing Lab Newsletter* 29.8 (2005): 1–6. Print.

———. "Into the City We Go: Establishing the SLCC Community Writing Center." *Writing Lab Newsletter* 27.6 (2003): 11–13. Print.

———. "SLCC Community Writing Center Development: Report of Spring 2000 Reassigned Time." 17 Apr. 2000. TS. Unpublished report to SLCC Administration.

———. "When the Community Writes: Re-envisioning the SLCC DiverseCity Writing Series." *Reflections* 5.1 (2006): 67–88. Print.

Rousculp, Tiffany, Clinton Gardner, Catherine Lund, Jeremy Remy, and Joanna Sewall. "Writing Assistant Training Program (CWC Version)." Unpublished training manual. [Orig. Fall 2001.] 4th rev., Jan. 2007. TS.

Ruffus, Stephen. Personal Interview. 21 Sept. 2010.

Russell, Bertrand. *Unpopular Essays*. New York: Simon, 1950. Print.

Ryan, Leigh, and Lisa Zimmerelli. *The Bedford Guide for Writing Tutors*, 5th ed. Boston: Bedford/St. Martin's, 2009. Print.

Salt Lake City Public Library. "About Us." *SLCPL.org*. Salt Lake City Public Library, 2003. Web. 7 July 2009.

"Salt Lake County Quick Facts from the US Census Bureau." *US Census Bureau*. US Census Bureau, State and County Quick Facts, 16 Aug. 2010. Web. 14 Oct. 2010.

Shaull, Richard. Foreword. *Pedagogy of the Oppressed*. By Paulo Freire. Trans. Myra Bergman Ramos. New York: Continuum, 2009. 29–34. Print.

Shor, Ira. *Empowering Education: Critical Teaching for Social Change.* Chicago: U of Chicago P, 1992. Print.

———. *When Students Have Power: Negotiating Authority in a Critical Pedagogy.* Chicago: U of Chicago P, 1996. Print.

Simin, Kenneth. Personal Interview. 15 Sept. 2010.

SLCC Community Writing Center. Salt Lake Community College, n.d. Web. 7 July 2010.

Street, Brian V. "Cross-Cultural Perspectives on Literacy." *Language and Literacy in Social Practice.* Ed. Janet Maybin. Clevedon, UK: Multilingual Matters, 1994. 139–50. Print.

Stuckey, J. Elspeth. *The Violence of Literacy.* Portsmouth, NH: Boynton/ Cook, 1991. Print.

"This I Believe—History." *National Public Radio.* Natl. Public Radio, 25 Apr. 2005. Web. 10 July 2010.

Trigger, Terry. Personal Interview. 28 Feb. 2011.

———. "President Bush, Stop Killing our Families!" *So They Said: Sine Cera, a DiverseCity Writing Series Anthology.* Ed. and comp. Elizabeth Coleman. Salt Lake City: SLCC Community Writing Center, 2007. 54. Print.

———. "To You, Dear." *There Is a Shorter View: Sine Cera, a DiverseCity Writing Series Anthology.* Ed. and comp. Joanna Sewall. Salt Lake City: SLCC Community Writing Center, 2005. 11. Print.

Trimbur, John. "Peer Tutoring: A Contradiction in Terms?" *Writing Center Journal* 7.2 (1987): 21–28. Print.

"USC Neighborhood Academic Initiative." *Communities.usc.edu.* U of Southern California, n.d. Web. 3 Oct. 2010.

Wallace, Ray, and Susan Lewis Wallace. "Growing Our Own: Writing Centers as Historically Fertile Fields for Professional Development." Murphy and Stay 45–51.

Warnock, John, and Tilly Warnock. "Liberatory Writing Centers: Restoring Authority to Writers." Olson 16–23.

Weisser, Christian R., and Sidney I. Dobrin, eds. *Ecocomposition: Theoretical and Pedagogical Approaches.* Albany: State U of New York P, 2001. Print.

Wellman, Jane V. "State Policy and Community College—Baccalaureate Transfer." National Center for Public Policy and Higher Education, and Institute for Higher Education Policy. National Center Report #02-6. Aug. 2002. Web. 22 Sept. 2013.

Wolf, Thomas. *Managing a Nonprofit Organization.* New York: Free Press. 2012.

Writing Across Communities (WAC) Alliance. University of New Mexico, n.d.. Web. 27 Oct. 2010.

Young, Deborah. Personal Interview. 28 Feb. 2011.

INDEX

184 / Index

AUTHOR

Tiffany Rousculp is associate professor of English at Salt Lake Community College in Utah where she teaches composition, linguistics, and sociolinguistics courses. She is the founding director of the SLCC Community Writing Center.

OTHER BOOKS IN THE CCCC STUDIES IN WRITING & RHETORIC SERIES

This book was typeset in Garamond and Frutiger by Barbara Frazier.
Typefaces used on the cover include Adobe Garamond and Formata.
The book was printed on 55-lb. Natural Offset paper
by Versa Press, Inc.